Routledge Library Editions

ALTERNATIVE SYSTEMS OF BUSINESS ORGANIZATION AND OF WORKERS' REMUNERATION

ECONOMICS

KEYNESIAN & POST-KEYNESIAN ECONOMICS
In 11 Volumes

I	Keynesian Economics	*Coddington*
II	Theories of the Bargaining Process	*Coddington*
III	The Social Science Imperialists	*Harcourt*
IV	On Political Economists and Modern Political Economy	*Sardoni*
V	Essays in the Theory of Economic Fluctuations	*Kalecki*
VI	Theory of Economic Dynamics	*Kalecki*
VII	Monetary Theory and Public Policy	*Kurihara*
VIII	Applied Dynamic Economics	*Kurihara*
IX	Post Keynesian Economics	*Kurihara*
X	Alternative Systems of Business Organization and of Workers' Remuneration	*Meade*
XI	Expectation, Enterprise and Profit	*Shackle*

ALTERNATIVE SYSTEMS OF BUSINESS ORGANIZATION AND OF WORKERS' REMUNERATION

J E MEADE

Routledge
Taylor & Francis Group
LONDON AND NEW YORK

First published in 1986

Reprinted in 2003 by
Routledge
2 Park Square, Milton Park, Abingdon, Oxfordshire OX14 4RN
or
270 Madison Avenue, New York, NY 10016

First issued in paperback 2010

Routledge is an imprint of the Taylor & Francis Group

British Library Cataloguing in Publication Data
A CIP catalogue record for this book
is available from the British Library

Alternative Systems of Business Organization
and of Workers' Remuneration
ISBN 978-0-415-31377-3 (hbk)
ISBN 978-0-415-60790-2 (pbk)

Miniset: Keynesian & Post-Keynesian Economics

Series: Routledge Library Editions – Economics

Alternative Systems of Business Organization and of Workers' Remuneration

J. E. Meade
University of Cambridge

London
ALLEN & UNWIN
Boston Sydney

**Allen & Unwin (Publishers) Ltd,
40 Museum Street, London WC1A 1LU, UK**

Allen & Unwin (Publishers) Ltd,
Park Lane, Hemel Hempstead, Herts HP2 4TE, UK

Allen & Unwin, Inc.,
8 Winchester Place, Winchester, Mass. 01890, USA

Allen & Unwin (Australia) Ltd,
8 Napier Street, North Sydney, NSW 2060, Australia

First published in 1986

British Library Cataloguing in Publication Data

Meade, J. E.
Alternative systems of business organization and of workers' remuneration.
1. Capitalism
I. Title
330.12'2 HB501
ISBN 0–04–331112–1

Library of Congress Cataloging-in-Publication Data

Meade, J. E. (James Edward), 1907–
Alternative systems of business organization and of workers' remuneration.
1. Competition, Imperfect—Mathematical models.
2. Unemployment—Effect of inflation on—Mathematical models. 3. Wages—Mathematical models. I. Title.
HB238.M4 1986 330'.1 85–26734
ISBN 0–04–331112–1 (alk. paper)

Contents

Preface

The models of various forms of economy which are presented in this book owe their origin and inspiration wholly to the work of Professor Martin L. Weitzman of the Massachusetts Institute of Technology. In particular in an article on 'Increasing Returns and the Foundations of Unemployment Theory' published in the *Economic Journal* for December 1982, he presented a simple macromodel of imperfect competition, that is to say of an economy in which at the micro level product differentiation was combined with increasing returns to scale. Subsequently, in an article on 'Some Macro–economic Implications of Alternative Compensation Systems' published in the *Economic Journal* for December 1983, he used his model of imperfect competition to analyse the effects on output and employment of different methods of compensating the factors for their contribution to the firm's output.

The exercises in the present volume are nothing more than a restatement and, in one or two particulars, a development of the Weitzman apparatus. For example, in the model of imperfect competition I have used a somewhat different (and in my view preferable) way of measuring the value of the differentiation between two products and I have used a different production function which distinguishes between the factors labour and capital. I have then applied the model to some forms of compensation to the factors which Professor Weitzman did not cover in his article on this subject; in particular I have applied it to what I call 'Non–Discriminating Labour Co–operatives' and 'Discriminating Labour–Capital Partnerships' as well as to the Capitalist Wage Economy and the Capitalist Sharing Economy, the two forms on which Professor Weitzman concentrated his attention.

In writing this book I have benefited from an extensive correspondence with Professor Weitzman; but he must not be held responsible for any of the particular assumptions used, or conclusions reached, in this book. In what follows I shall not make any further references to my indebtedness to Professor Weitzman; indeed, such references would clutter up practically every page that follows. I state here simply once and for all that his two articles caused this book to be written and that it is basically an exposition of various applications of his models.

A major purpose of Professor Weitzman's work was to assess the effectiveness of different forms of compensation for work done as a means of coping with the problem of stagflation, that is to say with the problem of reducing unemployment without leading to an inflation of money costs and prices. This is exactly my interest in studying these matters; and the present book is a sequel to my work on wage–fixing[1] which is a part of the project on stagflation on which, with the support of the Economic and Social Research Council, I and my colleagues have been working in Cambridge.

I am much indebted to John Flemming who read the whole book in typescript and prepared numerous comments on it. I have made extensive use of these comments and in particular have modified my treatment of Labour–Capital Partnerships as a result of them. But he is in no way responsible for my final judgement about the various possibilities; indeed, I have reason to believe that he does not fully accept them. My treatment of Labour–Capital Partnerships has also been much modified as a result of discussions of my proposals in seminars at the London School of Economics and Churchill College, Cambridge. I am also indebted to Martin Weale for various helpful criticisms.

The members of the typing pool of the Department of Applied Economics have treated the manuscript of this book in their usual efficient and friendly manner for which I am most grateful.

I want to thank my wife for her patient support during the concentrated process of work on this tedious book.

Department of Applied Economics J. E. MEADE
Cambridge
June 1985

[1] J. E. Meade, *Stagflation, Vol. 1, Wage–Fixing* (London: Allen & Unwin, 1982), and *Wage–Fixing Revisited*, Occasional Paper 72 (London: Institute of Economic Affairs 1985).

CHAPTER 1

Introduction

The purpose of this book is to examine the relationship between employment and money rates of pay in conditions of imperfect competition, when the level of total money expenditures on the products of labour is controlled by suitable financial policies on what I have called New Keynesian principles. Above all the purpose is to examine how the choice between different forms of business organization may in these conditions affect this relationship between employment and rates of pay. For this inquiry a very simple model of an imperfectly competitive economy is constructed and is then examined in operation with different organizational forms for the competing firms.

There are in fact a very large number of structural forms which might be adopted by business enterprises.

(1) A first question is: who takes the decisions about output, employment, investment, selling prices etc? One could imagine a pure entrepreneur who hires the factors and tells them what to do, himself bearing the risks and living on the excess of sales proceeds over contractual costs. Such an entrepreneur might himself have invested his capital in the concern; and decisions may then be taken either directly by some or all of the capitalists who have invested funds in the concern, or by managers appointed to act in their interest. But there is nothing in the nature of things to prevent decisions being the function of some or all of the workers either directly or through appointed managers. Or one could have a mixed system in which it was a mixed bag of some or all of the capitalists and some or all of the workers who were directly or indirectly responsible for making the decisions.

(2) A second question is: what form does the compensation of a factor take? Thus a worker or a capitalist may be paid by a fixed wage or fixed interest; but alternatively he may receive a pre–agreed share of the enterprise's profit (i.e. a share of any excess of the firm's value–added over its fixed contractual costs for wage or interest payments); or he may receive a pre–agreed

share in the enterprise's value–added with some group bearing the profit or loss which then arises after subsequent payment of any contractual liabilities for fixed–wage or fixed–interest payments. There could be many mixtures and variations of these arrangements which can be combined in various ways with the distribution of the decision-making functions discussed in the preceding paragraph.

(3) A third set of questions is: how flexible are any contractual or agreed wage rates, rates of interest, share ratios of profits or of revenue received by labour and capital; and by what means are these compensation parameters set?

(4) A fourth set of issues which are to a large extent dependent upon the structural arrangements discussed under (1), (2) and (3) above, raises the question: who bears the risks of (i) fluctuations in the revenue of the enterprise which is available for distribution to the factors of production and/or (ii) fluctuations in the level of employment of the factors of production?

(5) A fifth, and as we will argue later, a most important question is: are all the units of any one factor of production necessarily compensated at the same rate if they are employed side by side in the same enterprise (the principle of non–discrimination), or is it permissible for some units to receive a higher compensation than others (the principle of discrimination)? We will deal with this issue later as it arises in each particular case. But the distinction is so important that it may be helpful at the outset to explain its basic meaning and implications. This is done in a numerical example in the Note at the end of this chapter.

As a devoted taxonomist, I set out on the present work with the intention of covering all possible cases. But it soon became clear to me that if one takes all possible combinations under (1), (2), (3), (4) and (5) above one has to deal with hundreds, if not thousands, of different possible ways of organizing business structures. I have therefore confined myself to examining four possible cases.[1]

[1] When I wrote my book on *Trade and Welfare* one critic (I believe it was Abba Lerner, but I cannot remember whether it was in print or by word of mouth) accused me of being a spoil–sport (or words to that effect) because my complete taxonomy had ruined the pitch for a generation of research students since I had left no alternative cases for analysis in their theses. I have carefully avoided this criticism in this volume.

(1) In Chapter III I examine the Capitalist Wage Enterprise, where it is a group of all or some of the owners of the capital who directly or indirectly through managers take all the business decisions, hire labour on the principle of non–discrimination at a uniform contractually fixed wage, hire some capital at fixed interest, and are compensated by any excess of the firm's value–added over these contractual costs.

(2) In Chapter IV I examine the Non–Discriminating Labour Co–operative where it is all the workers who take the decisions, hire capital at fixed interest, and are compensated by the excess of the firm's value–added over these contractual payments, this compensation being distributed on the principle of non–discrimination among all the workers.

(3) In Chapter V I examine the Capitalist Sharing Firm where it is some or all of the capitalists who take the business decisions, compensate labour in part at least by a pre–arranged share of the value–added or the profits of the firm, perhaps paying out in addition some amounts of wages and interest at pre–arranged fixed rates, and retain for themselves any residual of the firm's revenue, the compensations to labour being on the principle of non–discrimination.

(4) Finally in Chapter VI I examine Discriminating Labour–Capital Partnerships where it is a mixed bag of capitalists and workers who take the business decisions, compensate other work and capital on pre–agreed contractually fixed rates, and share out between them the residue of the firm's value–added on flexibly determined ratios, the distribution of this residue between them not being bound by the principle of non–discrimination.

The exercises in this book are also limited in a number of other ways. They are built on very simple and very restrictive assumptions about the production function of the firm, about the similarities of all firms, and about marketing conditions and the factors determining consumers' choice. It is hoped that they do nevertheless serve to illustrate some of the important basic relationships between product differentiation, increasing returns to scale, and the choice of institutional structure of the firm. But there is, I fear, no rigorous examination of the question how far the conclusions reached have general validity and how far they depend essentially upon the particularities of the assumptions made about the form of production function or of consumers' choice or upon other aspects of the great simplifications of reality made for the construction of these simple models.

The exercises are also limited in the questions which they ask about the different institutional structures. To take one example, they do try to show what determines the price of a product to the producer (p) and the ratio (ρ) of that price to the 'cost' of the product to the consumer; and they also analyse the situation in terms of the money wage rate (w). But except in one case (see Section (d) of Chapter IV) they do not raise questions about the real value of the wage rate. The reader can however easily construct the answer to such questions by putting the available building bricks together to examine, for example, the value of the real wage ($w\rho/p$). The exercises are in fact based on rather mechanical, precise models designed merely to show how the system works and thus to enable the reader to construct for himself or herself answers to the particular questions which he or she wishes to raise.

There is yet another basic limitation. These exercises are exercises in the comparison between different steady states. They assume, for example, that the total money expenditure upon the net output of the economy is controlled by governmental (i.e. monetary and fiscal) policy and that the economy has reached an equilibrium against the background of this constant money national income and expenditure. Questions of growth and of lags of response of output to prices, of employment to output, of wages to employment, and so on, occurring as a result of some original exogenous shock, simply do not arise. The exercises compare one stationary steady state with another, without examining the dynamic path of the movement from the one such state to another. In fact one of the main questions to ask about the relative merits of different institutional organizations is how well they cope with the dynamics of change. Indeed, a main, perhaps the main claim, made by Professor Weitzman for the principle of the Share Economy[1] is that it meets a fluctuation in demand not by a fluctuation in employment and output but by a fluctuation in money price and money income. The exercises in this book are not well designed to examine profoundly the essence of this claim, though they do give the opportunity

[1] Martin L. Weitzman, *The Share Economy: Conquering Stagflation* (Harvard University Press, 1984).

for some *obiter dicta* on issues of this sort which are not, I believe, totally lacking in support from the analysis of the steady states. (See Section (h) of Chapter V).

For much the same reason the models which follow in the main body of this book are not well designed to deal with problems concerned with attitudes to risk and thus with the effects of different forms of business organization on the amount of risk and the response to risk of the various economic agents. Once again it has been possible for some *obiter dicta* to be made on some of the obvious points which arise in this connection. It is hoped that these are illuminating and helpful; but the field remains wide open for further more basic and more sophisticated research.

Finally, these exercises do not deal at all with the psychological, political, emotional attitudes which may be influenced by the choice of institutional organization of the firm. Revenue– or profit–sharing and participation in decision–making may have important effects upon industrial relations, upon incentives to work effectively and upon the quality of management, and thus upon productivity and the success or failure of the enterprise, quite apart from possible more far–reaching effects on ultimate attitudes to social and economic policies. None of these more indirect effects is taken into account in assessing in these exercises the merits and demerits of different systems. The exercises do, of course, take into account the effect of the response of economic agents to a change in the immediate market situation which confronts them and in this sense do take account of differences in incentives in the different systems. But they do so in a mechanical way without assuming that a different institutional milieu has an effect upon the basic underlying attitude of the agent to any given market situation.

There is thus a large range of issues with which the following exercises make no claim to cope. Nevertheless one may perhaps end this introductory chapter with a short justification for their publication in spite of all these limitations. They do, it is claimed, draw attention to certain simple, mechanistic, underlying economic relationships between market incentives and outcomes for economies which share in common the two basic features of imperfect competition (namely, product differentiation and increasing returns to scale) but which differ in their institutional organization. If their message rings at all true, they do in fact show beyond all reasonable doubt that the choice of institutional structure is of basic importance to society.

Note to Chapter I on the Principles of Discrimination and Non–Discrimination[1]

The distinction between the principles of discrimination and of non–discrimination is illustrated in the numerical example given in Table I.1.

Consider an ordinary company which issues 100 £1 shares and uses the proceeeds to purchase 100 machines which cost £1 a piece, which together produce a net revenue of £20 for the company. If the market rate of discount of earnings on such shares is 10 per cent, these shares will be valued in the market at £2 a share, the high productivity of the machines leading to a capital gain from £1 to £2 a share.

In view of its success the company decides to install another 100 machines, which as before cost £1 a piece. To finance this investment the company needs to issue only an additional 50 shares at the stock exchange value of £2 a share. The additional machines, however, add only £10 to the company's net revenue because of the cost involved in the expansion of the market for the company's product. The firm's

Table I.1

	Number of Shares of Nominal Value of £1 (a)	*Value of Shares £* (b)	*number of Machines with Constant Replacement Cost of £1 a Machine* (c)	*Revenue Produced £* (d)	*Discount Rate %* (e)
Original Issue of Shares	100	—	100	£20	10%
		£200 ←			
New Issue of Shares	+50	+£100	+100	+£10	—
Total	150	£300	200	£30	10%
		£300 ←			

[1] For an earlier discussion of the distinction between discrimination and non-discrimination in the employment of a factor of production, see J. E. Meade 'The theory of labour-managed firms and of profit sharing', *Economic Journal*, special issue (March, 1972), pp. 402–28.

total revenue is now £30 which, discounted at the market rate of 10 per cent, implies that the 150 shares will now be worth £300 on the stock exchange, so that the market value of a share remains unchanged at £2. The company is now in equilibrium.

This history illustrates the fact that the principle of discrimination is applied to the investment of machines in the company. The capitalists who 'installed' (i.e. financed the purchase of) the first 100 machines own 2/3 of the total shares while the later capitalists who 'installed' the second 100 machines own only 1/3 of the total shares. The second group put as much resources into the concern as the first group, but they receive only half as great a rate of 'pay' on their machines or, what comes to the same thing, they receive the average revenue on only 66.6 machines although they financed the purchase of 100 machines.

There is nothing in the nature of things which requires the application of the principle of discrimination to capital investment. Consider a case which can be represented by columns (c) and (d) of Table I.1 where Antonio ventures a ship costing 100 ducats on a trading venture which will earn 20 ducats. Suppose he invites Bassanio to join the enterprise with a second ship costing 100 ducats, it being realized that a fleet of two ships will earn only 30 ducats. They may well agree that as each is providing the same number of ships they will share the 30 ducats equally between them. But in this case, of course, Antonio by inviting Bassanio to join the enterprise will have reduced his own earnings from 20 ducats (on a single ship) to 15 ducats (the average earned on each of two ships); and he may well be discouraged from doing so if this principle of non–discrimination between the rates of pay is applied to the enterprise.

Exactly similar distinctions can be drawn between different arrangements for the employment of labour, which can again be illustrated by columns (c) and (d) of Table I.1, if for '100 machines' one reads 'one man'. The first worker adds £20 to the value of output, the second worker adds only £10, and the average per worker is thus £15 a head. In the normal capitalist company labour will be hired at a single non–discriminating rate of pay. If this were £10 a man, the company illustrated in the Table would employ both men, paying on the non–discriminating principle £10 to each man, and thus retaining an income of £10 (£30 – £20) to finance its other costs or to keep as a pure profit.

But suppose that the Table illustrated the number of members in a

Labour Co–operative or partnership of some form. The first member would earn £20. If he admitted a second member on the discriminating principle, he could keep the £20 on agreement with the second member that he should receive only half as much of the co–operative's revenue as the first member. If the principle of non–discrimination were observed, then the first member by admitting the second member would experience a reduction in his income from £20 to £15. If for that reason he was unwilling to expand the operations of the co–operative, expansion would have to rely on the setting up of a separate competing co–operative by the excluded second member. Such competition due to the entry of a new business would in turn tend to reduce the average income of both separate concerns to £15 each.

Note to Chapter I on Notation

In the following chapters the activities of a firm will be expressed in lower–case letters such as x (output), l (labour employed), k (capital equipment in use), and p (selling price of the product). When the economy is in equilibrium, all firms will be operating at the same values of these variables. When it seems desirable to underline the fact that the argument at a particular point is concerned with variations of activity by a single firm with independently given and constant levels of activity for the other firms, the relevant variables will be marked with a bar, such as $\bar{x}$, $\bar{l}$, $\bar{k}$, and $\bar{p}$.

The number of firms is expressed by m. Upper–case letters such as X ($= mx$), L ($= ml$), and K ($= mk$) measure the levels for the economy as a whole of the corresponding lower–case variables for the single firm. $\bar{m}$ represents the final equilibrium number of firms when there is no incentive for new firms to enter or for existing firms to leave the market.

Variables with a hat refer to welfare or socially optimal values. Thus $\hat{x}$ and $\hat{p}$ refer respectively to amounts (or qualities) of product enjoyed by consumers and to the price of the product as it enters into the cost of living, while $\hat{m}$ measures the socially desirable number of firms required for the best satisfaction of consumers' needs.

Variables marked with a star such as L^* and K^* represent target values of the variable in question.

w measures the fixed wage rate paid to a firm's workers, w' measures the inclusive rate of pay earned by a firm's workers (i.e. fixed wage plus any agreed share of profit or revenue), and w''

measures any relevant standard of earnings set by factors outside the control of the firm, against which the adequacy of the firm's w' must be judged.

Similarly h measures the fixed rate of 'hire–charge' paid by a firm for the use of a unit of capital equipment, h' measures the inclusive return earned in a firm on a unit of capital equipment (i.e. including any element of share of revenue or profit accruing to the owners of the capital), and h'' measures the comparable return on a unit of capital available outside the firm, against which the adequacy of the firm's return must be judged.

$q = xp - w''l - h''k$ measures the total profit made by a firm, i.e. the excess of its revenue over and above the outside comparable earnings of the factors. q_k and q_l measure the division of this profit between that received by the capitalists and that received by the wage earners, with $q_k = xp - w'l - h''k$ (i.e. revenue of the firm less the inclusive payment of labour and less what the capital could earn outisde the firm) and $q_l = w'l - w''l$ so that $q = q_k + q_l$.

From these definitions we can deduce

$$w' = w'' + \frac{q_l}{l}$$ (actual pay = outside pay plus profit per worker)

$$= \frac{xp - h'k}{l}$$ (revenue less payments to capital per worker)

where

$$h' = h'' + \frac{q_k}{k}$$ (actual receipts = outside receipts plus profit per unit of capital)

$$= \frac{xp - w'l}{k}$$ (revenue less payments to workers per unit of capital).

We define q_s as the structural profit of a firm where $q_s = xp - \lambda l - \varkappa k$, i.e. as the excess of revenue over what the cost of the factors would be if they were paid rewards equal to their marginal revenue products (λ in the case of labour and $\varkappa$ in the case of capital). This structural profit is the profit that is made possible if the imperfect market structure allows such a high average price mark–up over and above marginal revenue, while the increasing–returns production requires such a moderate average cost mark–up over and above the marginal cost, that there is an excess of average revenue over average cost when marginal revenue is equated to marginal cost.

Finally we define as accounting profit $q_a = xp - wl - hk$ which is the excess of revenue over the sum of the fixed–wage element in the pay of the workers and the fixed–interest element in the hire–charge for capital equipment.

From the above definitions it can be seen that

$$q - q_s = (\lambda - w'')l + (x - h'')k,$$

i.e. the excess of the factors' marginal revenue products over what the factors could earn elsewhere, and that

$$q_a - q = (w'' - w)l + (h'' - h)k,$$

i.e. the excess of what the factors could earn elsewhere over the fixed–wage or fixed–interest elements in their inclusive pay, so that

$$q_a - q_s = (\lambda - w)l + (x - h)k.$$

Other variables will be defined as and when they are introduced.

CHAPTER II

The Structure of the Model

(a) The Market Structure

The basic feature of monopolistic competition is the combination of production in conditions of increasing returns to scale with a differentiation between products which are competitive with each other but with less than infinite substitutability between them in consumers' choices.

The present section models this degree of differentiation between products more or less exactly on the lines suggested by Professor Weitzman.[1] He considers consumers' tastes for different varieties of product as distributed evenly round a circle as in Figure II.a.1. We suppose that if a consumer with a need at point b has to satisfy that need with a product designed expressly to satisfy a need at point a, then the distance *D* between the two points a and b will determine the reduction of usefulness of the product to the consumer below what it would have been if the product had taken the form expressly designed to satisfy his need at point b. The even spread of tastes would imply that there would be the same loss involved wherever points a and b were positioned on the circle, provided that the distance *D* between them were unchanged, as between a to b and b to c in Figure II.a.1. This sort of model rests, of course, upon the simple assumption that there is only one dimension to the differentiation between products.

There is in fact one form of differentiation between products which can very readily be expressed in the form of distribution round a circle. If the circle represents an actual geographical circular road round which consumers dwell in a continuous even spread, and if there is in fact only one form of product, then the distance *D* will measure the actual geographical distance between factory (at a) and consumer (at b). If the cost of transport depends solely upon the distance over which the product is transported and can be measured in terms of the product itself, then the model is complete and exact.

[1] M. L. Weitzman, 'Increasing returns and the foundations of unemployment theory', *Economic Journal* (December, 1982).

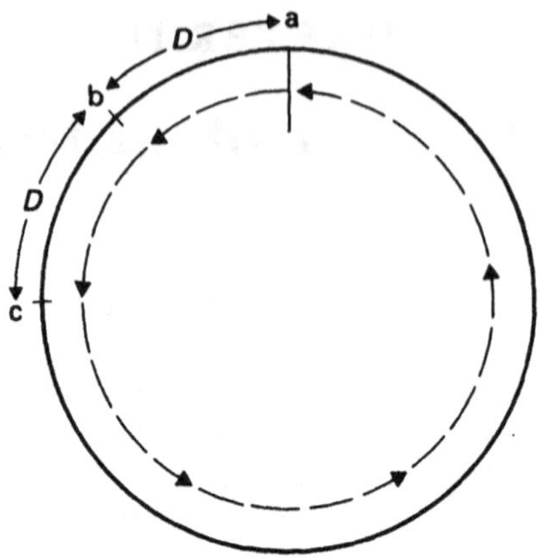

Figure II.a.1

One unit of product at factory gate a would provide one unit of consumption good at point a, but ends up as an amount of consumption good at consumption point b equal to one unit less the loss of product in transport over a distance *D*. In the rest of this book we will confine ourselves to the analysis in these terms of differentiation of a single product by geographical distance between point of production and point of consumption.[1]

We assume then a geographical circle round which the total of consumer's expenditure of money on the single product is evenly spread. In general we can justify this assumption of an even spread of money expenditures around the circle by assuming that there is an even spread of every kind of consumer round the circle. For example, employed workers are evenly spread, unemployed workers are evenly spread, and capital ownership is evenly spread in dwellings round the

[1] It is not easy to think of any other single dimension of differentiation which could strictly satisfy the above conditions. It is possible to overcome the problem of defining a unit of 'product' which is the same in 'quantity' for all goods however different they may be in 'quality' (e.g. chalk and cheese) by assuming all products to be subject to the same production technology and by reference to the amounts of the various products which would be produced in each case by the same given amount of factors of production. But it is extremely difficult to imagine a single quality (other than location) such that as one proceeded the whole way round the circle the quality would change by the same amount in the same direction at each step, but would nevertheless end up with no change from its starting point at a when one had completed the passage round the circle, as indicated by the dashed line in Figure II.a.1. Perhaps a cross with the cross–bar gradually changing its angle with the upright from 0° to 360° would also satisfy this condition.

circle. If in equilibrium every employed worker received the same wage, every unemployed worker the same benefit, and every unit of capital the same return, in equilibrium consumption expenditure would be evenly spread round the circle whatever happened to the distribution of income between these three classes of recipients of income.

While there is a continuous spread of expenditure all round the circle, there will be only a finite number of factories producing the product at a finite number of points round the circle. With increasing returns to scale production by means of an indefinitely large number of tiny factories spread continuously around the circle would be excessively costly. In equilibrium, however, this finite number of firms will be placed at equal distances from each other round the circle, simply because each firm will attempt to protect itself from the competition of neighbouring firms by getting as far away as possible from its neighbours in order to gain the maximum possible protection through the cost of transport of its neighbour's products into its own market.

If H measures the length of the circle's circumference and m measures the finite number of firms, then in equilibrium each firm will cover a market span equal to H/m. In equilibrium each firm will be selling the same amount (x) and charging the same factory–gate price (p).

With increasing returns to scale each firm would produce more than this x if it were not for the fact that in order to do so it would have to cut its price (p) in order to invade the market of the neighbouring firms. It will produce until its marginal revenue has fallen to equality with its marginal cost. The market analysis consists in determining what is the relationship between the individual firm's average revenue or price (p) and its marginal revenue or, in other words, what is the price elasticity of demand with which a firm assumes itself to be confronted in the market.

Consider a firm producing at point a in Figure II.a.2 with its close rivals producing at points b and c. Suppose firms b and c to be charging the price p, but that firm a reduces its price to $\bar{p} < p$, so that it invades the markets of its rivals and extends its market share from H/m to $2D$. At the points e and f consumers must be indifferent between the more expensive but nearer products of firms b and c and the less expensive but more distant product of firm a. Firm a's product will have travelled a distance D while firm b's and firm c's products

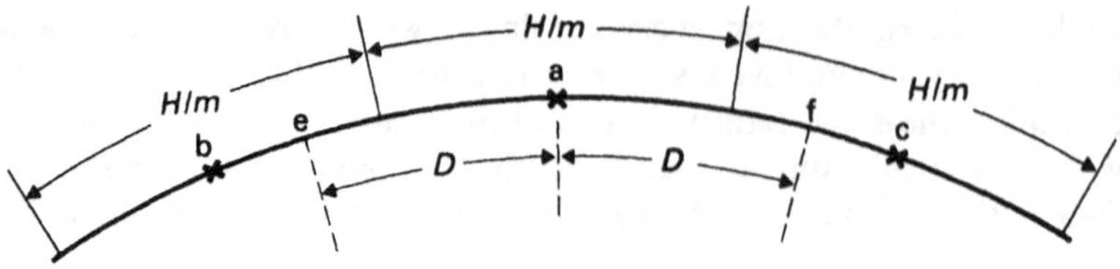

Figure II.a.2

will have travelled a distance of only $H/m - D$. If $T(D)$ represented the cost in terms of the product of carrying a unit of a product over a distance D, then the consumers at e and f would be indifferent between their two nearest sources of supply only if

$$\frac{\bar{p}}{p} = \frac{1 - T(D)}{1 - T(H/m - D)}. \qquad \text{II.a.1}$$

There are different ways in which the transport cost might be modelled. One way to express it would be to write

$$T(D) = \mu D, \qquad \text{II.a.2}$$

where μ would measure the amount of product needed to transport a unit of product over a unit of distance.

But this does not allow for the fact that as the product was transported, the cost in terms of the product means that there remains less net product to be transported. A more satisfactory assumption might, therefore, be that

$$T(D) = 1 - e^{-\mu D}, \qquad \text{II.a.3}$$

which represents the fact that as a unit of product is transported it decays in amount at a rate equal to μD so that after transport over a distance D only $e^{-\mu D}$ is left and the amount lost in transport cost is therefore $1 - e^{-\mu D}$. Moreover, if the formula in (II.a.2) were adopted, the transport of a unit of product over a distance equal to $1/\mu$ would mean that there was no product remaining to be carried. The formula in (II.a.3) means that, however great the distance, there remains something of value, however small, after deduction of transport costs. This formulation is for this reason probably preferable if one wants to apply the model by analogy to cases of differentiation by 'quality' of product other than geographical locality. We shall accordingly use it throughout the rest of this essay.

Using the expression for $T(D)$ in (II.a.3) we could rewrite (II.a.1) as

$$\bar{p}e^{-\mu(H/m-D)} = pe^{-\mu D} \qquad \text{II.a.4}$$

so that with p constant

$$\frac{d\bar{p}}{\bar{p}} = -2\mu\, dD. \qquad \text{II.a.5}$$

At the same time, if the total money expenditure by consumers is Y and if this is evenly spread round the circle, then a's total receipts ($\bar{x}\bar{p}$ where $\bar{x}$ is the firm's output and $\bar{p}$ its selling price at the factory gate, i.e. net of any transport costs)[1] will represent a fraction of total expenditures (Y) which is measured by the ratio of its market span to the whole circumference of the market circle, so that

$$\frac{\bar{x}\bar{p}}{Y} = \frac{2D}{H}. \qquad \text{II.a.6}$$

It follows that with Y constant

$$\frac{dD}{D} = \frac{d\bar{x}}{\bar{x}} + \frac{d\bar{p}}{\bar{p}}. \qquad \text{II.a.7}$$

[1] The consumers at point a and point e both spend £1 on the product. In each case the firm receives £1. The consumer at a receives £1/p units of x; but the consumer at point e for his £1 receives only $\{£1/p\}\{1 - T(D)\}$ units of x, so that the price to him including transport cost is $p/\{1 - T(D)\}$. We are assuming that the producer does not discriminate between the two consumers, although in the case of transport costs he might do so by insisting on selling to all consumers at the same delivered price (i.e. inclusive of transport costs). Thus the producer might charge a price of $p/\{1 - T(D)\}$ to the consumer at a, since the consumer at a would not be able to find a cheaper source of supply. It seems appropriate to assume that producers sell at the same factory–gate price to all consumers, if the model is intended to be used by analogy to cover varieties of quality of product as well as differences of transport cost. While it might be possible for a producer to discriminate between purchases by consumers at different geographical points, it would seem impossible for him to discriminate between a sale of green peas which was being bought because the consumer wanted green peas and a sale of green peas which was being bought because there were no blue peas on the market.

If we eliminate dD between (II.a.5 and 7) we obtain

$$\bar{\eta} \equiv -\frac{\bar{p}}{\bar{x}}\frac{\mathrm{d}\bar{x}}{\mathrm{d}\bar{p}} = 1 + \frac{1}{2\mu D}, \qquad \text{II.a.8}$$

where $\bar{\eta}$ is the elasticity of demand for its product which the firm expects to confront when it expands its market span to $2D$.

Using the familiar formula for the ratio of Average Revenue to Marginal Revenue we obtain

$$\frac{\text{Price}}{\text{Marginal Revenue}} = \frac{\bar{\eta}}{\bar{\eta} - 1} = 1 + 2\mu D = 1 + \bar{\pi}, \qquad \text{II.a.9}$$

where $\bar{\pi} = 2\mu D$ is the 'mark–up' of price over expected marginal revenue on the basis of which it will be conducting its operations over a market span of $2D$. It is to be noted from (II.a.8) that as D is increased $\bar{\eta}$ will fall and the level of sustainable price and profit mark–up will be reduced.

If and when both the economy and the firm are in equilibrium, we will have each firm spread evenly over the market circle with $xp = Y/m$. In this case from (II.a.6) we have $2D = H/m$ so that we can write

$$\frac{\text{Price}}{\text{Marginal Revenue}} = \frac{\eta}{\eta - 1} = 1 + \frac{\mu H}{m} = 1 + \pi. \qquad \text{II.a.10}^{1}$$

Thus in any equilibrium situation with marginal revenue = marginal cost, the term π can be regarded as a factor which in ordinary monopolistic–competition equilibrium measures the 'mark–up' of price on marginal cost.

The whole derivation of this elasticity of demand and this mark–up factor, quite apart from the particular form given in (II.a.9), depends in this model on firm a assuming that if it cuts its price its competitors will maintain their prices and geographical location unchanged. In fact, of course, they are likely to respond by some cut in their prices (which will reduce a's sales) and by some change of locality to distance themselves from a (which will help a's sales). One needs really to call

[1] If we had used (II.a.2) instead of (II.a.3) for the measure of costs we would have obtained $\eta = \frac{1}{2} + m/\mu H$ instead of $1 + m/\mu H$ and $\pi = \mu H/2m$ instead of $\mu H/m$.

in aid the theory of games. However the essential point in the model is simply to assume that for the individual firm with its equilibrium share of the market, the firm's behaviour will be governed on the basis of an assumed price elasticity of demand for its product *which depends solely upon the number m of competing firms in the monopolistically competitive market.* The greater the number of firms, the more intense the competition and the larger the assumed price elasticity of demand for its output.

(b) The Welfare Measure

In monopolistic competition there is something to be gained in total output by concentrating production on a small number of firms (to take advantage of the economies of scale) but something to be gained in quality of consumption by increasing the number of firms and thus increasing the range of choice of varieties of product. Any welfare measurement must take account of both factors.

This can be done in a straightforward manner in the present case in which product differentiation is simply a matter of transport costs which takes the form of an exponential decay of the product as it moves over a distance D. Thus one unit of product available at a given point of production is reduced to $e^{-\mu D}$ when it has been transported to a point of consumption over a distance D.

In Figure II.b.1, x is a firm's output which is sold at the factory gate at an even rate of xm/H to the purchasers who are spread evenly over its marked span H/m. At a distance D from the factory gate the rate of consumption will have fallen to $(xm/H)e^{-\mu D}$. In Figure II.b.1, the rectangle $xm/H \times H/2m = x/2$ measures that half of the firm's output which is sold to purchasers lying to the right of the factory gate. The area under the curve is

$$\frac{xm}{H}\int_0^{H/2m} e^{-\mu D}\,dD = \frac{xm}{\mu H}\frac{e^{\mu H/2m} - 1}{e^{\mu H/2m}}.$$

The ratio between this area and the rectangle $x/2$ is

$$\rho = \frac{2m}{\mu H}\frac{e^{\mu H/2m} - 1}{e^{\mu H/2m}}, \qquad \text{II.b.1}$$

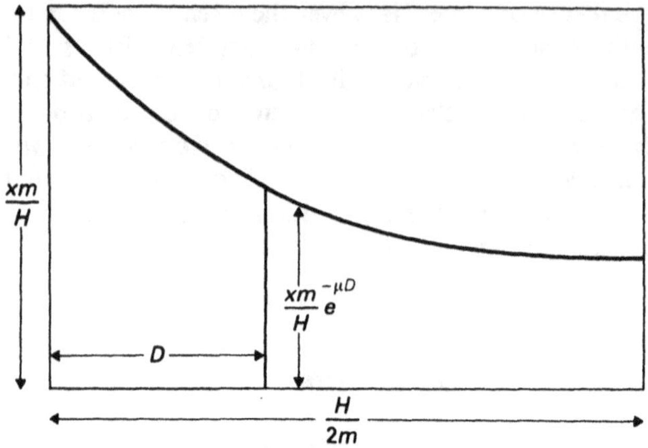

Figure II.b.1

where ρ measures the proportion of any produced output which actually reaches the consumer.

We will in what follows use the following notation: $\hat{x} = \rho x$ where x is a firm's output and $\hat{x}$ is the amount of the output which reaches the consumer. Correspondingly we will use $\hat{p} = p/\rho$[1] where p measures the factory–gate price of output and $\hat{p}$ measures the **average** price charged to consumers for the product. Consumers near the point of production will have a cost of living less than $\hat{p}$, while those on the edge of the factory's market will be charged (inclusive of transport costs) more than $\hat{p}$.

It can be seen from (II.b.1) that ρ is a function only of m if μ and H are given, and by differentiation of (II.b.1) one obtains

$$\frac{\mathrm{d}\rho}{\rho} = \frac{\mathrm{d}m}{m} \frac{e^{\mu H/2m} - 1 - \mu H/2m}{e^{\mu H/2m} - 1}. \qquad \text{II.b.2}$$

Since from (II.a.10) $\mu H/m \equiv \pi$ and measures the profit mark–up in industry, observation of the real world suggests that π is likely to take a value of less than unity. If as a result we disregard in the expansion of $e^{\mu H/2m}$ all terms less than $(\mu H/2m)^2 \frac{1}{2!}$ we derive from (II.b.2) the

[1] $\hat{x}\hat{p}$ measures the total amount spent by consumers while xp measures the total amount received by producers. But $\hat{x}\hat{p} = xp$, so that $\hat{p} = p(x/\hat{x}) = p/\rho$

following approximate value for $d\rho/\rho$, namely

$$\frac{d\rho}{\rho} \simeq \frac{\pi}{4+\pi}\frac{dm}{m}.^{1} \qquad \text{II.b.3}$$

We will use this approximate value of $d\rho/\rho$ in later sections of this essay.

(c) The Production Function

Of the two basic features of monopolistic competition we described a very simple model of product differentiation in Section (a). In this section we turn to the second basic feature, namely increasing returns to scale in production, which we model in the equation

$$x = k^{\alpha}l^{\beta} \qquad \text{II.c.1}$$

with $0 < \beta < 1$, $0 < \alpha < 1$ and $\alpha + \beta > 1$, where x is a firm's output, k is its total stock of capital equipment, and l is the amount of labour employed by the firm.

Increasing returns to scale are represented by the fact that $\alpha + \beta > 1$.[2]

[1] The degree of inaccuracy introduced by this approximation may be judged from the following comparison of true and approximate values

$\pi = \frac{\mu H}{m}$	$\frac{d\rho}{\rho} \div \frac{dm}{m}$ True Value	Approximate Value
%		
200	.418	.333
100	.230	.200
50	.120	.111
20	.049	.048

[2] The present book has been drafted and redrafted in terms of different ways of modelling increasing returns to scale including (1) $x = (k-f)^{\alpha}l^{1-\alpha}$ (2) $x = k^{\alpha}(l-f)^{1-\alpha}$ and (3) $x = k^{\alpha}l^{1-\alpha} - f$, where f is in each case a fixed 'overhead cost' element. The form $x = k^{\alpha}l^{\beta}$ has the great attraction of simplicity; but, as will be seen later (cf. V.d.7), it has the effect in certain exercises of setting no limit to the growth in the number of firms.

Differentiation of II.c.1 gives

$$\frac{\partial x}{\partial k} = \alpha \frac{x}{k} \qquad \text{II.c.2}$$

and

$$\frac{\partial x}{\partial l} = \beta \frac{x}{l}, \qquad \text{II.c.3}$$

which express the marginal products of the two factors k and l.

This production function also yields:

$$\left.\begin{aligned} \frac{\partial^2 x}{\partial k^2} &= -(1-\alpha)\alpha \frac{x}{k^2} < 0 \\ \frac{\partial^2 x}{\partial l^2} &= -(1-\beta)\beta \frac{x}{l^2} < 0 \end{aligned}\right\} \qquad \text{II.c.4}$$

$$\left.\begin{aligned} \frac{\partial (x/k)}{\partial k} &= -(1-\alpha)\frac{x}{k^2} < 0 \\ \frac{\partial (x/l)}{\partial l} &= -(1-\beta)\frac{x}{l^2} < 0 \end{aligned}\right\} \qquad \text{II.c.5}$$

$$\frac{\partial^2 x}{\partial l \partial k} = \frac{\alpha\beta}{kl} x > 0 \qquad \text{II.c.6}$$

$$\left.\begin{aligned} \frac{\partial (x/k)}{\partial l} &= \frac{\beta}{kl} x > 0 \\ \frac{\partial (x/l)}{\partial k} &= \frac{\alpha}{kl} x > 0 \end{aligned}\right\} \qquad \text{II.c.7}$$

With α and β each having a value between 0 and 1, equations (II.c.4 to 7) state that an increase in any one factor will reduce both the marginal and the average product of the factor, but will raise both the marginal and average product of the other factor. These assumptions of a well behaved production formation are necessary conditions for much that follows.

If we write w for the pay of a unit of labour and h for the cost of 'hiring' a unit of capital equipment, we can express a firm's average cost of production by

$$AC = \frac{hk + wl}{x}. \qquad \text{II.c.8}$$

The marginal cost of raising output by using more capital can be expressed as

$$MKC = h\frac{\partial k}{\partial x} = \frac{hk}{\alpha x} \qquad \text{II.c.9}$$

and by using more labour as

$$MLC = w\frac{\partial l}{\partial x} = \frac{wl}{\beta x}. \qquad \text{II.c.10}$$

But in equilibrium in order to minimize cost the firm will use labour and capital in proportions which equate the resulting marginal costs so that from (II.c.9 and 10) we obtain

$$hk = \frac{\alpha}{\beta}wl \qquad \text{II.c.11}$$

and substituting in (II.c.8)

$$AC = \frac{wl}{x}\left(1 + \frac{\alpha}{\beta}\right). \qquad \text{II.c.12}$$

Using (II.c.10 and 12) we obtain

$$\frac{AC}{MC} = \alpha + \beta \equiv 1 + \gamma$$

or

$$\frac{AC - MC}{MC} = \alpha + \beta - 1 = \gamma \qquad \text{II.c.13}$$

where $1 + \gamma$ measures the ratio of average cost to marginal cost.

In other words, γ measures the 'mark–up' on marginal cost needed to cover average cost, just as π in (II.a.10) measures the 'mark–up' on marginal revenue needed to cover average revenue or price.

The relationship between $\pi = \mu H/m$ and $\gamma = \alpha + \beta - 1$ will play an important role in the following exercises. It is to be noted that an increase in m will lower π because it increases competition and allows a smaller 'mark–up' of selling price, whereas with our present production function γ remains unchanged whatever happens to output or the number of firms. This is the basic simplification introduced by our choice of production function.

On the assumption that the production function is as described in this section and that the market conditions are as described in Section (a) of this chapter, we can now derive expressions for the marginal revenue product of each factor.

Using (II.a.10) and (II.c.2 and 3) we obtain

$$\mathrm{d}(xp) = \frac{xp}{k}\frac{\alpha}{1+\pi}\,\mathrm{d}k + \frac{xp}{l}\frac{\beta}{1+\pi}\,\mathrm{d}l. \qquad \text{II.c.14}$$

From which it is clear that

$$\frac{\partial(xp)}{\partial k} = \frac{xp}{k}\frac{\alpha}{1+\pi} = x \qquad \text{II.c.15}$$

and

$$\frac{\partial(xp)}{\partial l} = \frac{xp}{l}\frac{\beta}{1+\pi} = \lambda$$

where x and λ are the marginal revenue products of k and l respectively.

It may be noted that $\alpha/(1+\pi)$ is the proportion of the firm's revenue which would be needed to pay capital its marginal revenue product and $\beta/(1+\pi)$ is the proportion of the revenue needed to pay labour its marginal revenue product. These proportions play an important role in the analysis in later chapters of this book.

(d) The Demand–Management Structure

In the analysis of the macro–economic aspects of monopolistic competition a basic question is what determines the level of employment or unemployment of resources. Before we can examine this question it is necessary to construct a simple model of what determines the total demand for the products of industry.

Many different simple models of the factors determining the level of total demand can be constructed. We will construct one such model on what may be called New Keynesian Demand–Management principles, by which we mean that the Government adopts a set of financial policies designed to stabilize the total *money* national income (Y), using interest rate policy primarily to influence the total expenditures on the product of industry for the purpose of capital investment and fiscal policy primarily for controlling the total level of consumption expenditures. We will assume that the Government does not itself purchase any of the products of industry.

We can write

$$Y = C + I \text{ with } I = p\left\{m\frac{\mathrm{d}k}{\mathrm{d}t} + k\frac{\mathrm{d}m}{\mathrm{d}t}\right\} \qquad \text{II.d.1}$$

to represent the fact that total money expenditures consist of, and thus the total of money incomes (Y) is derived from, money expenditures on consumption (C) plus money expenditures on capital investment (I), this latter item consisting of money expenditures by existing firms on new investment ($pm(\mathrm{d}k/\mathrm{d}t)$) and of money expenditures on capital equipment for the setting up of new firms ($pk(\mathrm{d}m/\mathrm{d}t)$).

The investment function for an existing firm may be thought of in the very simple form of

$$p\frac{\mathrm{d}k}{\mathrm{d}t} = \phi(x, h) \qquad \text{II.d.2}$$

where, from (II.c.15), $x = \{xp/k\}\{\alpha/(1+\pi)\}$ measures the marginal revenue product of capital and h expresses the cost of 'hiring' capital. In stationary equilibrium we may assume

$$h = \frac{xp}{k}\frac{\alpha}{1+\pi} \qquad \text{II.d.3}$$

An interesting and important point arises in the determination of h. If there is only one product, each firm will in fact avoid transport costs by accumulating a stock of its own output for capital investment purposes. But the opportunity cost of its own output is not the market price at which it can sell it (p) but only the marginal revenue which it forgoes by refraining from selling it ($p/(1+\pi)$). Thus if it can borrow money at a rate of interest i, its opportunity-cost 'hire' of a unit of real capital is

$$h = \frac{ip}{1+\pi}, \qquad \text{II.d.4}$$

in which case (II.d.3) becomes

$$i = \alpha\frac{x}{k}. \qquad \text{II.d.5}$$

The outcome is, however, quite different if one is considering the case of differentiation of products by quality of product rather than by location and cost of transport. In this case one considers consumers as desiring a mix of products evenly spread all round the circle of tastes described in Figure II.a.1 and as having for a given expenditure a more 'efficient' package of goods if the variety of products is greater. Similarly one may assume that for use of products for investment purposes a mix with greater variety is more 'efficient' as an instrument of production than the same quantity with less variety. In other words, just as one uses $\hat{x}, = x\rho$ (see the discussion of II.b.1) as the 'efficient' unit of consumption, so one uses $\hat{k} = k\rho$ instead of k as the efficiency unit for capital equipments with $\hat{p} = p/\rho$ as the market price of this efficiency unit of capital equipment.

The formula for investment in (II.d.1) remains unchanged because, with $\hat{p} = p/\rho$ and $\hat{k} = k\rho$, $\hat{p}(\mathrm{d}\hat{k}/\mathrm{d}t) = p(\mathrm{d}k/\mathrm{d}t)$ and $\hat{p}\hat{k} = pk$. But the expression in (II.d.3) for the marginal revenue product of efficiency units of capital becomes

$$\frac{xp}{\hat{k}}\frac{\alpha}{1+\pi} = \frac{x\hat{p}}{k}\frac{\alpha}{1+\pi}$$

and the opportunity cost of hiring a unit of capital which must now be bought in the market from other producers becomes

$$h = i\hat{p}, \qquad \text{II.d.6}$$

so that the equilibrium equality between marginal revenue product and cost of hire becomes

$$i=\frac{x}{k}\frac{\alpha}{1+\pi}, \qquad \text{II.d.7}$$

which replaces (II.d.5).

In fact in the rest of this book we shall concern ourselves only with comparisons between different equilibrium states in all of which the total capital equipment actually employed is the same, namely $K=K^*$ (if we are dealing with transport cost differentiation) or $\hat{K}=\hat{K}^*$ (if we are dealing with quality variation). We shall assume that this result is brought about by governmental monetary policy which so adjusts the rate of interest (i) as to influence the hire–charge for capital (h) in such a way that a firm's demand for capital equipment (k), when multiplied by the number of firms (m), is equal to the given 'target' amount of capital equipment to be employed ($K=K^*$). For example, when the number of firms grows, then during the process of change the cost of hiring capital equipment is raised by the monetary authorities to the extent needed to make existing firms release capital equipment for the new firms; and this is conducted in terms of the relation between i and $\alpha x/k$ in the case of a constant K^* and in terms of the relation between i and $\alpha x/\hat{k}$ in the case of a constant $\hat{K}^*$.

The result of a governmental monetary policy of this kind which effectively keeps the total demand for capital equipment at a constant 'target' level could have been achieved perhaps more easily by making the simple assumption that, for one reason or another, there was a fixed amount of a given factor (K^* or $\hat{K}^*$) available to be used and that firms competed for its use with the result that there emerged a hire–charge (h) which equated demand to the fixed supply of this factor. We have chosen to tell the rather more elaborate story not because it is necessary for the comparative static exercises which follow, but because it may help to keep open the way to anyone who wishes to dynamize a model of this kind.

A similar point can be made about the preceding discussion of the distinction between the factors affecting the level of the hire–charge (h) in the case of transport costs and in the case of quality differences (c.f. II.d.4 and 6). This distinction could be important if any attempt were made to turn the present model into a dynamic model of growth. In fact they constitute a digression in the present essay, throughout which we assume I in (II.d.1) to be zero and K to be constant at K^*. The following analysis would be totally unchanged in form if we replaced (II.c.1) with the production function $x = \hat{k}^{\alpha} l^{\beta}$ and assumed that the government used its control of i and so of h so as to keep $\hat{K}$ constant at $\hat{K}^*$. In both cases (II.d.3) remains valid, though the same level of h would require a different level of i.

We proceed then with $I = 0$ and in this case equation (II.d.1) becomes

$$Y = C, \qquad \text{II.d.8}$$

which implies that the Government adopts a fiscal policy which ensures that all income is spent on consumption. We can model such a fiscal demand–management policy in the following way.[1]

Suppose that the private consumption function were

$$C = c_1(Y + T) + c_2(pK^* + Z), \qquad \text{II.d.9}$$

where T measures the net current fiscal transfers from the Government to the private sector (i.e the excess of the sum of interest paid on the national debt and social security or other similar positive transfer payments to the private sector over revenue raised in the form of taxes on income) and where Z measures the value of the total outstanding national debt. Thus private consumption expenditures are modelled as being increased by c_1 times any increase in spendable incomes and by c_2 times any increase in total private wealth.

We assume then that the government successfully sets T at any time in any given conditions at a level which, in the light of (II.d.8 and 9), will keep Y at a policy determined level Y^*. From (II.d.8 and 9) it can be seen that this involves setting T at the level

$$T = \frac{Y^*(1 - c_1) - c_2(pK^* + Z)}{c_1}. \qquad \text{II.d.10}$$

But, on the assumption that all national debt is incurred in forms such as Treasury Bills on which changes in the rate of interest do not cause capital gains or losses, the growth in the national debt will be

$$\frac{dZ}{dt} = T. \qquad \text{II.d.11}$$

[1] I am indebted to Martin Weale for suggesting to me the following procedure.

From this it follows that, if initially a positive $T > 0$ were needed to keep Y at the target level Y^*, there will be a growing Z. But from (II.d.10) it is clear that, with a growing Z, a declining T will be needed to keep Y on target. Thus T will approach zero, as Z approaches $Y^*(1-c_1)/c_2 - pK^*$.

Thus Y can be stabilized at a planned level Y^* by means of a fiscal policy which in the stationary equilibrium will involve an ultimate national debt of

$$Z = \frac{Y^*(1-c_1)}{c_2} - pK^*. \qquad \text{II.d.12}$$

It would, of course, always have been possible by interest rate policy, through the operation of h on the incentive to invest to have induced a planned value of K^* such that $pK^* = Y^*(1-c_1)/c_2$, so that the ultimate national debt was zero.

In the rest of this essay we shall be interested only in the effect of variations in Y on the assumption of a constant level of K^*. The preceding simple model of how a New Keynesian policy, relying on monetary policy primarily to control the accumulation of capital and on fiscal policy primarily to control consumption expenditures, might result in given levels for Y and K is, of course, only one out of many possible stories. The remaining chapters of this book will treat Y and K^* as variables set in this way at predetermined planned levels through fiscal and monetary policies. The basic analysis would, however, remain valid for other stories about the factors determining Y and K^*.

CHAPTER III

The Capitalist Wage Economy

(a) The Nature of the Capitalist Wage Economy

The first type of institutional set–up of the firm which we examine in this chapter is the familiar case in which the owners of the capital equipment take the decisions about output, employment, prices etc. and bear the risks of the enterprise, hiring the labour which they employ at a uniform money wage rate.

The owners of the capital equipment may not have financed the whole of that equipment out of their own funds; they may have borrowed funds at a fixed rate of interest in order to purchase some of their equipment. All that is assumed is that some part of the equipment has been financed by capitalist entrepreneurs (the owners of the equity or 'ordinary shares') who take the decisions about the firm's activities and receive their income in the form of the residual which is left over after deducting the wage bill and any debt interest from the net revenue of the firm.

It is to be noted that in the meaning of the terms discussed in Chapter I the Capitalist Wage Economy treats capital inputs on a Discriminating basis but labour inputs on a Non-Discriminating basis.

Thus suppose that £100 is raised by the flotation of 100 Ordinary Shares to purchase 100 units of machinery at £1 a unit. Suppose the firm does well and earns on those machines a rate of reward which is twice as great as the current rate of interest so that the firm's ordinary shares go up in value from £100 to £200. Suppose now that it issues 50 additional ordinary shares to raise another £100 to double its real capital equipment from 100 to 200 machines. The original shareholders now own 2/3 and the new shareholders 1/3 of the 150 shares which have been issued and thus command 2/3 and 1/3 respectively of the product of the machinery which has been installed, though in fact they are each of them responsible for having put into the business the same number of machines, namely in each case 100 out of the total of 200. In a successful business 'owners' of the newly installed machines are not treated as favourably as the 'owners' of the original equipment.[1] In contrast to this, all the workers are paid the same wage for the same job however long or however short the period for which they have been employed. New hands are not taken on at a lower rate of pay than old hands. Everyone is paid the same rate for the job. Thus a capitalist who finances the purchase of a new machine will not necessarily receive the same income as another capitalist who has already financed the purchase of a machine, whereas a worker who takes on a new job will receive the same wage as another worker who is already employed on a similar job.

We may measure the capitalists' profit made in the firm ($\bar{q}_K$) by the expression

$$\bar{q}_K = \bar{x}\bar{p} - h\bar{k} - w\bar{l}, \qquad \text{III.a.1}$$

where $\bar{x}$ is the output which the entrepreneurs in this firm decide to put on the market, with $\bar{p}$ the price at which they expect to sell that output and $\bar{k}$ and $\bar{l}$ the amounts of capital equipment and labour which they need to produce that output. $\bar{q}_K$, $\bar{x}$, $\bar{p}$, $\bar{k}$, and $\bar{l}$ are the variables which they can directly or indirectly vary as a result of their decisions. h and w, the prices which they must pay for the factors, are set by forces outside the control of the individual firm.

Throughout this chapter we operate with $w = w' = w''$. That is to say, the whole of a firm's pay to a worker (w') consists of a fixed wage (w) and this is set at a level (w'') determined by factors outside the control of the firm.

Similarly, $h = h''$. That is to say, the firm pays a hire–charge for the

[1] A particular example of this distinction between the treatment of existing and of new owners is to be found in the case of a 'rights' issue of ordinary shares. Suppose that in a successful firm an investment of £100 in a new machine would produce an addition to profit of £20 a year (a return of 20 per cent per annum), while at the same time the market rate of return on the company's ordinary shares was only 10 per cent per annum. If an amount of the company's shares, worth £100 at current market prices, were issued to new shareholders, these new shareholders would receive a dividend income of £10 leaving another £10 of the profit to be added to the dividends of the existing shareholders. Alternatively the gain to the existing shareholders might take the form of a 'rights' issue. In this case the existing shareholders would be given the opportunity of taking part (in proportion to each shareholder's existing holding of the company's shares) in the purchase for £100 of an amount of the company's shares worth £200 at current market prices, since the £20 profit earned on the new machine would be sufficient to finance the 10 per cent market rate of return on £200 worth of the company's shares. In this case the existing shareholders would enjoy the gain not in the form of an addition to the dividend on their existing shares but in the form of purchasing for £100 an amount of shares worth £200, an offer which would not be open to new shareholders.

use of a unit of capital equipment which takes the form of a fixed rent (h) which in turn is set by monetary forces at a level (h'') beyond the firm's control. In so far as the capitalist entrepreneurs have invested some of their own funds at risk in the business we must treat them as paying themselves the market rate of return in the form of a fixed rent ($h = h''$) and accounting for the remainder of any return in their investment in their profit (q_k).

As we show later in this section (III.a.5 and 6), it will be profitable for the firm to expand its employment of labour and capital until the marginal revenue products are equal to the prices of the factors, i.e. until $w = \lambda$ and $h = x$. It follows, therefore, that in equilibrium in terms of the notation explained in the Note at the end of Chapter I we will throughout the present chapter have

$$q = q_k = q_a = q_s$$

$$q_l = 0$$

and

$$h' = h + \frac{q_k}{k}.$$

Thus in the Capitalist Wage Economy in equilibrium we need think only in tems of one sort of profit, namely the structural profit (q_s) due to the interaction between the structure of the imperfect market for the sale of the product and the structure of the increasing–returns–to–scale production function, the whole of which profit will accrue to the capitalists (q_k).

By differentiation of (III.a.1) we have

$$\mathrm{d}\bar{q}_k = \bar{x}\bar{p}\left(\frac{\mathrm{d}\bar{x}}{\bar{x}} + \frac{\mathrm{d}\bar{p}}{\bar{p}}\right) - h\bar{k}\frac{\mathrm{d}\bar{k}}{\bar{k}} - w\bar{l}\frac{\mathrm{d}\bar{l}}{\bar{l}}. \qquad \text{III.a.2}$$

But from (II.a.9) and (II.c.2 and 3)

$$\frac{\mathrm{d}\bar{x}}{\bar{x}} + \frac{\mathrm{d}\bar{p}}{\bar{p}} = \frac{1}{1+\bar{\pi}}\frac{\mathrm{d}\bar{x}}{\bar{x}}$$

$$= \frac{1}{1+\bar{\pi}}\left\{\alpha\frac{\mathrm{d}\bar{k}}{\bar{k}} + \beta\frac{\mathrm{d}\bar{l}}{\bar{l}}\right\}. \qquad \text{III.a.3}$$

It follows from (III.a.2 and 3) that

$$d\bar{q}_k = \left(\frac{\bar{x}\bar{p}}{1+\bar{\pi}}\alpha - h\bar{k}\right)\frac{d\bar{k}}{\bar{k}} + \left(\frac{\bar{x}\bar{p}}{1+\bar{\pi}}\beta - w\bar{l}\right)\frac{d\bar{l}}{\bar{l}}, \qquad \text{III.a.4}$$

so that maximization of profit involves increasing $\bar{k}$ until

$$\bar{k} = \frac{\bar{x}\bar{p}}{h}\frac{\alpha}{1+\bar{\pi}} \qquad \text{III.a.5}$$

and increasing $\bar{l}$ until

$$\bar{l} = \frac{\bar{x}\bar{p}}{w}\frac{\beta}{1+\bar{\pi}}. \qquad \text{III.a.6}$$

(b) The Capitalist Wage Economy with Unemployment and a Given Number of Firms

In this section we assume that the money wage rate is exogenously set (e.g. by a national trade union–employer organization bargain) and that it is set at a sufficiently high level that, given the level at which the government is maintaining total money expenditures on the products of labour (Y), the level of employment is below the full employment level ($L < L^*$). We assume also in this section that the number of firms (m) is exogenously set and is not influenced by the level of profit. Moreover, we assume, as we shall throughout the rest of this book, that the government through its interest rate policy manages so to control the cost of hiring a unit of capital equipment (h) that the total amount of capital equipment in use remains constant at $K = K^*$.

The equilibrium position for the economy, in which each firm is producing the same output (x), employing the same amounts of capital (k) and of labour (l) and selling at the same factory–gate price (p), can be described by equations (III.b.1 to 8).

(III.b.1) states that each firm will earn a revenue (xp) which represents its equal share of total money expenditure (Y). (III.b.2) repeats the production function from (II.c.1). (III.b.3) states that each firm will employ its equal share of the available capital equipment (K^*). (III.b.4) repeats (III.a.6) and states that each firm will employ labour (l) up to the point at which the money wage (w) is equal to the value of its marginal revenue product. (III.b.5) states the rate at which

$$xp = Y/m \qquad \text{III.b.1}$$

$$x = k^{\alpha} l^{\beta} \qquad 2$$

$$k = \frac{K^*}{m} \qquad 3$$

$$l = \frac{xp}{w} \frac{\beta}{1+\pi} \qquad 4$$

$$h = \frac{xp}{k} \frac{\alpha}{1+\pi} \qquad 5$$

$$X = mx \qquad 6$$

$$L = ml \qquad 7$$

$$q = q_K = xp - hk - wl \qquad 8$$

Equations III.b.1 to 8

the government must set the hire for capital equipment (h) in order to induce each firm to use its quota of the available amount of capital equipment (k) and no more. (III.b.6 and 7) express the level of total output and employment. (III.b.8) repeats for the final equilibrium position the definition of a firm's profit given in (III.a.1).

These eight equations can be rearranged as in equations (III.b.9 to 16) in which case the dependent variables k, l, x, p, h, X, L and q_K are expressed in terms of the constants K^*, α, β, μ, and H and in terms of the institutional–policy parameters Y, w, and m.

The equations (III.b.17 to 24) then show how the eight dependent variables would be affected by changes in the three institutional–policy variables, Y, w, and m.

It is clear from (III.b.9 and 17) that with a constant total amount of capital equipment in employment (K^*) the amount employed by any one firm (k) must fall in the same proportion as any rise in the number of firms (m) over which the capital must be spread.

In (III.b.10 and 18) Y/w measures the level of 'effective demand' in the sense that it measures the real purchasing power of total money expenditures over labour (i.e. in terms of wage units) and

$$k = \frac{K^*}{m} \qquad \text{III.b.9}$$

$$l = \frac{Y}{mw} \frac{\beta}{1+\pi} \qquad 10$$

$$x = \left(\frac{K^*}{m}\right)^{\alpha} \left(\frac{Y}{mw} \frac{\beta}{1+\pi}\right)^{\beta} \qquad 11$$

$$p = \frac{Y}{m}\left(\frac{K^*}{m}\right)^{-\alpha} \left(\frac{Y}{mw} \frac{\beta}{1+\pi}\right)^{-\beta} \qquad 12$$

$$h = \frac{Y}{K^*} \frac{\alpha}{1+\pi} \qquad 13$$

$$X = m\left(\frac{K^*}{m}\right)^{\alpha} \left(\frac{Y}{mw} \frac{\beta}{1+\pi}\right)^{\beta} \qquad 14$$

$$L = \frac{Y}{w} \frac{\beta}{1+\pi} \qquad 15$$

$$q = \frac{Y}{m} \frac{\pi - \gamma}{1+\pi} \qquad 16$$

where $\pi = \mu H/m$ and $\gamma = \alpha + \beta - 1$

Equations III.b.9 to 16

$(\mathrm{d}Y/Y) - (\mathrm{d}w/w)$, therefore, measures the proportionate increase in effective demand.

In what follows we shall treat $\mathrm{d}Y/Y$ as being determined independently from $\mathrm{d}w/w$ for the reasons explained in Section (d) of Chapter II. We assume governmental fiscal policy to determine Y and independent labour–market features to determine w. This is contrary to the pure Keynesian assumption that a fall in the money wage will, or at least may, lead simply to a fall in all prices and so to an equal proportionate fall in Y. It is of course, simple to construct a model in which this would be so. Suppose a fixed proportion c of income Y were spent and that there were exogenous expenditures of pG, where G represented an exogenous *real* demand for goods for government

$$\frac{dk}{k} = -\frac{dm}{m} \qquad \text{III.b.17}$$

$$\frac{dl}{l} = \frac{dY}{Y} - \frac{dw}{w} - \frac{1}{1+\pi}\frac{dm}{m} \qquad 18$$

$$\frac{dx}{x} = \beta\left(\frac{dY}{Y} - \frac{dw}{w}\right) - \left(1 + \gamma - \beta\frac{\pi}{1+\pi}\right)\frac{dm}{m} \qquad 19$$

$$\frac{dp}{p} = (1-\beta)\frac{dY}{Y} + \beta\frac{dw}{w} + \left(\gamma - \beta\frac{\pi}{1+\pi}\right)\frac{dm}{m} \qquad 20$$

$$\frac{dh}{h} = \frac{dY}{Y} + \frac{\pi}{1+\pi}\frac{dm}{m} \qquad 21$$

$$\frac{dL}{L} = \frac{dY}{Y} - \frac{dw}{w} + \frac{\pi}{1+\pi}\frac{dm}{m} \qquad 22$$

$$\frac{dX}{X} = \beta\left(\frac{dY}{Y} - \frac{dw}{w}\right) - \left(\gamma - \beta\frac{\pi}{1+\pi}\right)\frac{dm}{m} \qquad 23$$

$$\frac{dq}{Y/m} = \frac{\pi-\gamma}{1+\pi}\left(\frac{dY}{Y} - \frac{dm}{m}\right) - \frac{\pi(1+\gamma)}{(1+\pi)^2}\frac{dm}{m} \qquad 24$$

Equations III.b.17 to 24

use, for export, or for domestic investment. We would then have

$$Y = cY + pG = \frac{pG}{1-c} \qquad \text{III.b.25}$$

so that

$$\frac{dY}{Y} = \frac{dG}{G} + \frac{dp}{p}$$

or, using (III.b.20) with $dm/m = 0$,

$$\frac{dY}{Y} = \frac{dG}{G} + (1-\beta)\frac{dY}{Y} + \beta\frac{dw}{w} = \frac{1}{\beta}\frac{dG}{G} + \frac{dw}{w}. \qquad \text{III.b.26}$$

In this case with $dG/G = 0$, it would be true that a reduction in w

would cause an equal proportionate fall in Y, so that there would be no increase in effective demand. This illustrates the way in which the analysis in this book could be used to illustrate demand–management structures other than the New Keynesian structure assumed in Section (d) of Chapter II.

From (III.b.18) it is clear that with any given number of firms employment will increase in proportion to the increase in effective demand. This results from the fact that the combination of the assumed production function with a constant number of firms (and thus with the mark–up $\pi = \mu H/m$ constant) results in labour always receiving the same proportion of income. This is shown by writing (III.b.10) in the form $mwl/Y = \beta/(1+\pi)$. With a constant proportion of expenditure going to the wage bill, employment rises in the same ratio as 'effective demand' measured in terms of wage units.

An increase in the number of firms will decrease employment in each individual firm in so far as it involves spreading a given amount of employment over more firms. But since the increase in the number of firms, by increasing competition, will reduce the profit mark–up on costs, there will be a shift of revenue from profits to wages. Equation (III.b.18) accordingly shows that the proportionate decrease in employment in the firm will be equal to only $1/(1+\pi)$ times the proportionate increase in the number of firms. In the case of total employment, as shown in (III.b.22) there will be the favourable effect of a shift of revenues away from profit onto wages $(+(\pi/[1+\pi])(\mathrm{d}m/m))$ without the adverse spreading effect which affected the result in (III.b.18).

From (III.b.19) it is clear that an increase in effective demand will, through an equal proportionate increase in the firm's employment, lead to a proportionate increase in its output equal to β times the increase in effective demand. An increase in the number of firms will have three effects on the firm's output: (1) it will spread output over a larger number of firms $(-\mathrm{d}m/m)$; (2) it will cause a loss of economies of scale by spreading resources over a larger number of firms, $(-\gamma\,\mathrm{d}m/m)$; but (3) it will increase competition and cause a shift of revenue away from profits and thus lead to the employment of more labour $(+\beta(\pi/[1+\pi])(\mathrm{d}m/m))$. The proportionate effect on total output, shown in (III.b.22), will be the same as the effect on output per firm without the adverse spreading effect mentioned under (1) above.

The price effects shown in (III.b.20) can be best understood by using $p = Y/X$ and thus considering $\mathrm{d}p/p = \mathrm{d}Y/Y - \mathrm{d}X/X$, using the discussion of $\mathrm{d}X/X$ as given in the previous paragraph.

The expression for q in equation (III.b.16) has a straightforward interpretation. π measures the proportional excess of selling price over marginal revenue; and γ (the index of increasing returns to scale) measures the proportional excess of average cost over marginal cost. With marginal revenue equal to marginal cost, $(\pi - \gamma)/(1 + \pi)$ represents the excess of average revenue over average cost relative to average revenue, i.e. the proportion of revenue (Y/m) which is available for profit.

In equation (III.b.24) we express the change in a firm's profit ($\mathrm{d}q$) relative to the firm's total revenue (Y/m) rather than to the profit itself in order to cover the case where $q = 0$. The first term in this equation shows how a change in the total revenue of a firm $(\mathrm{d}Y/Y - \mathrm{d}m/m)$ will affect the profit simply by changing the scale of its total revenue; and the second term shows how an increase in the number of firms $(\mathrm{d}m/m)$ will reduce the share of this total revenue which goes to profits because the increased competition due to the increased number of competing firms will lead to a reduction in the profit mark–up (π).

All of the above equations for prices and outputs have been in terms of prices (p) and outputs (x and X) at the factory gate. But, as has been argued in connection with Figure II.b.1, any welfare implications should be considered in terms of the prices ($\hat{p}$) and amounts ($\hat{x}$ and $\hat{X}$) concerned at the points of consumption.

We have from (II.b.1)

$$\hat{X} = \rho X \qquad \text{III.b.27}$$

and

$$\hat{p} = p/\rho \qquad \text{III.b.28}$$

which, using (II.b.3) and (III.b.20 and 23) with Y and w constant, gives

$$\frac{\partial \hat{X}}{\hat{X}} = -\left(\gamma - \frac{\beta\pi}{1+\pi} - \frac{\pi}{4+\pi}\right)\frac{\partial m}{m} \qquad \text{III.b.29}$$

and

$$\frac{\partial \hat{p}}{\hat{p}} = +\left(\gamma - \beta\frac{\pi}{1+\pi} - \frac{\pi}{4+\pi}\right)\frac{\partial m}{m}. \qquad \text{III.b.30}$$

A numerical example may help. Suppose $\gamma = .2$, $\beta = .7$, and $\pi = .3$, then $\gamma - \beta(\pi/[1+\pi]) = .04$ and $\pi/(4+\pi) = .07$. At the factory gate the loss of output due to the loss of economies of scale would be less than fully offset by the increase in output due to increased employment; but this net loss at the factory gate would be more than offset by the saving in transport costs or by the increased variety of products. We would have

$$\frac{dX}{X} = -.04\frac{dm}{m} \text{ with } \frac{d\hat{X}}{\hat{X}} = +0.3\frac{dm}{m}$$

and

$$\frac{dp}{p} = +.04\frac{dm}{m} \text{ with } \frac{d\hat{p}}{\hat{p}} = -0.3\frac{dm}{m}.$$

In the rest of this essay we shall confine ourselves to an analysis of prices and outputs at the factory gate. The reader is left to consider prices and consumption at the place of consumption by adding $(\pi/[4+\pi])(dm/m)$ to the changes in factory–gate outputs and subtracting $(\pi/[4+\pi])(dm/m)$ from the changes in factory–gate prices.

(c) The Capitalist Wage Economy with Unemployment and a Market–Determined Number of Firms

In this section we continue the analysis with the same assumptions as in the previous section except that the number of firms is no longer treated as given exogenously.

Accordingly we ask what determines the number of firms. We assume that firms will disappear if $q < 0$. The simple Chamberlinian assumption is that new firms will enter so long as $q > 0$, so that full long–term equilibrium will require the number of firms to be such that $q = 0$.

The assumption that new firms will be attracted into production so long as $q > 0$ ignores the 'costs' incurred by a new firm entering a market. Such 'costs' may take two forms.

In the first place, if increasing returns to scale are very important relative to the size of the market, the numbers of firms in the market will be small. In this case the entry of one more firm will have a significant effect upon the profitability of existing firms and so of the new firm. A firm's profitability is expressed in (III.b.16) as $q = (Y/m)([\pi - \gamma]/[1+\pi])$. An increase in the number m will reduce this figure in two ways. (1) The total expenditure in the market (Y) will be distributed over a larger number of firms (m) so that each firm's total revenue (Y/m) will be lowered. (2) The greater number of firms will intensify inter–firm competition and as a result the mark–up ($\pi = \mu H/m$) will be reduced (See II.a.9), with a resulting reduction of profit per firm. A numerical example may help. If $Y = 400$, and $\gamma = .1$ then there would be the following relationships between m and the components of q:

m	Y/m	π	q
8	50.0	.125	1.111
9	44.4	.111	0.444
10	40.0	.100	0.000

With eight firms in the market, profit per firm would be $1.\dot{1}$. A ninth firm would reduce this to $0.\dot{4}$, and this reduction is the equivalent of a cost of entry for the ninth firm if it is considering entering a market in which the ruling profit is $1.\dot{1}$ per firm.

If, however, increasing returns to scale are not so important relative to the size of the market, there will be room for a large number of competing firms. In this case one more additional firm will cause a negligible change in Y/m and in $\mu H/m$ so that the entry of new firms will not appreciably break the market. We shall in fact assume in what follows that the number of firms is sufficiently large for this aspect of costs of entry to be realistically neglected.[1]

But there is a second form of costs of entry. The q which is determined in (III.b.16) is the equilibrium q which arises when the firms are evenly distributed around the circle of tastes. But a new firm coming in has to squeeze itself in between two existing firms. For a time there will be savage competition between the three firms, the two existing firms cutting their prices to meet the challenge of the new firm. The

[1] Differentiation in respect of m in equations (III.b.17 to 24) is really inappropriate except in those cases in which increasing returns to scale are sufficiently unimportant to allow for a really large number of firms. In the real world, increasing returns to scale in relation to the size of the market are important for some products and unimportant for others.

two neighbouring firms will then move round the circle away from the intruder, causing them to compete closely with the next two firms on each side of the turbulent span on the circle. And so on, until in the long run the firms are once again evenly distributed round the circle. Even if there were in fact a very large number of firms so that after this turmoil the effect of a new entrant on the prevailing level of q would be small, the once–for–all costs of entry may be substantial so that new entrants would in fact be attracted only if q were a positive figure which exceeded the equivalent of a market rate of yield on the once–for–all entry costs. The level of these costs of entry would depend *inter alia* upon the costs involved by the existing firms in moving from one point to another on the circle of tastes and upon the dynamic processes of adjustment which are not the subject of this book. In a note at the end of this section we outline a way in which these setting–up costs might be analysed. We will, however, neglect them in the rest of this book.

If we assume that new firms are set up so long as $q > 0$, we will end with an equilibrium number of firms with

$$\tilde{q} = 0 \qquad \text{III.c.1}$$

which, using (III.a.16), implies

$$\tilde{\pi} = \gamma \qquad \text{III.c.2}$$

so that using

$$\pi = \frac{\mu H}{m}$$

$$\tilde{m} = \frac{\mu H}{\gamma} \qquad \text{III.c.3}$$

where $\tilde{m}$ and $\tilde{\pi}$ are the equilibrium values of m and π when a firm's revenue just covers its costs.

This implication of the model is easily understood. With increasing returns to scale average cost will always exceed marginal cost and γ measures the 'mark–up' on marginal cost which is needed to cover average cost. With imperfect competition average revenue will always exceed marginal revenue and π measures the 'mark–up' of average revenue on marginal revenue. If to maximize profit marginal revenue is equated to marginal costs, this means that with $\pi > \gamma$ average revenue will exceed average cost and a net profit will be made. In our model γ is a constant,[1] but π depends upon the expected elasticity of a firm's demand curve which depends in turn upon the degree of competition in the market which, in our model, is assumed in turn to depend solely upon the number of competing firms. Thus an increase in m reduces the market 'mark–up', π, down to equality with the cost 'mark–up', γ.

The level of the firm's profit (q) is, of course, dependent upon the level of expenditure on the firm's products (Y/m) as can be seen from (III.b.16). But the number of firms ($\tilde{m}$) and so the mark–up ($\tilde{\pi}$)

$$k = \frac{K^*\gamma}{\mu H} \qquad \text{III.c.4}$$

$$l = \frac{Y}{w}\frac{\gamma\beta}{\mu H(1+\gamma)} \qquad 5$$

$$x = \left(\frac{\gamma}{\mu H}\right)^{1+\gamma}(K^*)^{\alpha}\left(\frac{Y}{w}\frac{\beta}{1+\gamma}\right)^{\beta} \qquad 6$$

$$p = Y\left(\frac{\mu H}{\gamma}\right)^{\gamma}(K^*)^{-\alpha}\left(\frac{Y}{w}\frac{\beta}{1+\gamma}\right)^{-\beta} \qquad 7$$

$$h = \frac{Y}{K^*}\frac{\alpha}{1+\gamma} \qquad 8$$

$$L = \frac{Y}{w}\frac{\beta}{1+\gamma} \qquad 9$$

$$X = \left(\frac{\gamma}{\mu H}\right)^{\gamma}(K^*)^{\alpha}\left(\frac{Y}{w}\frac{\beta}{1+\gamma}\right)^{\beta} \qquad 10$$

$$q = 0 \qquad 11$$

Equations III.c.4 to 11

[1] This is perhaps unrealistic. With an element of constant overhead cost (see footnote on page 19) the ratio of average cost to marginal cost would fall as output increased, so that γ would be a decreasing function of a firm's output, x.

which will reduce the profit per unit of expenditure on the firm's product to zero is unaffected by the absolute level of expenditure on the firm's product (Y/m).

The equations (III.b.9 to 16) can now be rewritten substituting in them $\mu H/\gamma$ for m and $1+\gamma$ for $1+\pi$ as in equations (III.c.4 to 11).

The equations (III.b.17 to 24) can be rewritten and greatly simplified. Since $\bar{m}$ is a constant which does not depend upon Y or w, all terms in $\mathrm{d}m/m$ can be omitted, as is done in equations (III.c.12 to 19). It can then be seen that employment goes up in the same proportion as effective demand $(\mathrm{d}Y/Y - \mathrm{d}w/w)$; that output goes up in a proportion which is β times the proportional increase in effective demand; and the price level goes up in a proportion equal to $(1-\beta)$ times the proportional increase in Y and β times the proportional increase in w.

$$\frac{\mathrm{d}k}{k} = 0 \qquad \text{III.c.12}$$

$$\frac{\mathrm{d}l}{l} = \frac{\mathrm{d}Y}{Y} - \frac{\mathrm{d}w}{w} \qquad 13$$

$$\frac{\mathrm{d}x}{x} = \beta\left(\frac{\mathrm{d}Y}{Y} - \frac{\mathrm{d}w}{w}\right) \qquad 14$$

$$\frac{\mathrm{d}p}{p} = (1-\beta)\frac{\mathrm{d}Y}{Y} + \beta\frac{\mathrm{d}w}{w} \qquad 15$$

$$\frac{\mathrm{d}h}{h} = \frac{\mathrm{d}Y}{Y} \qquad 16$$

$$\frac{\mathrm{d}L}{L} = \frac{\mathrm{d}Y}{Y} - \frac{\mathrm{d}w}{w} \qquad 17$$

$$\frac{\mathrm{d}X}{X} = \beta\left(\frac{\mathrm{d}Y}{Y} - \frac{\mathrm{d}w}{w}\right) \qquad 18$$

$$\frac{\mathrm{d}q}{Y/m} = 0 \qquad 19$$

Equations III.c.12 to 19

Note to Section (c) of Chapter III on the Cost of Entry of a New Firm

Suppose that a new firm will enter only if it has a prospect of making a profit or at least of covering its costs if it squeezes in half–way between two existing firms, while it assumes that those firms will go on producing where they are and will go on charging an unchanged factory price, p. In fact, of course, the existing firms are likely (1) to reduce their price in competition with the new comer but (2) to move away from him. The newcomer's neglect of (1) means that he is underestimating the cost of entry, while his neglect of (2) means that he is overestimating the cost of entry. These assumptions of unchanged behaviour by existing firms correspond to the assumptions made in connection with equation (II.a.4) for the derivation of the expected elasticity of demand for the products of an individual firm in the final equilibrium situation.

In Figure III.c.1, existing firms produce at b and c. The new firm sets up at a, covers a span of $2D$, and charges a price $\bar{p}$. Where it competes with the products of b and c, which cost p at points b and c, we must have

$$\frac{\bar{p}}{p} = \frac{1 - T(D)}{1 - T(H/2m - D)} = e^{\mu(H/2m - 2D)} \qquad \text{III.c.20}$$

if, as in (II.a.3), we assume $T(D) = 1 - e^{-\mu D}$.

If the new firm assumes p to be constant, differentiation of (III.c.20) gives

$$\frac{d\bar{p}}{\bar{p}} = -2\mu \, dD. \qquad \text{III.c.21}$$

With an equal spread of expenditure round the consumers' circle we

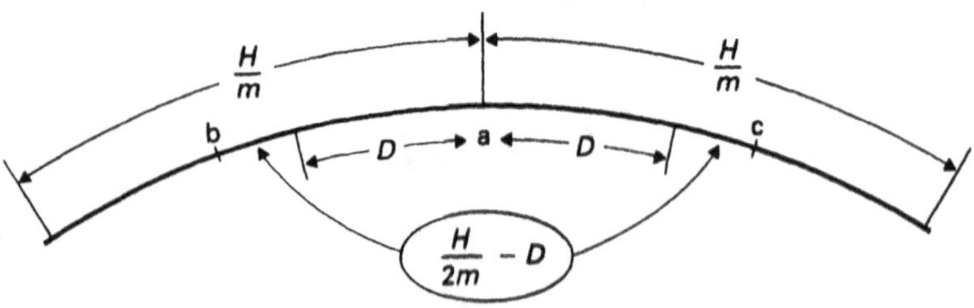

Figure III.c.1

have

$$\frac{\bar{x}\bar{p}}{Y} = \frac{2D}{H} \text{ (c.f. II.a.6)} \qquad \text{III.c.22}$$

and with Y and H constant we have

$$\frac{d\bar{x}}{\bar{x}} + \frac{d\bar{p}}{\bar{p}} = \frac{dD}{D}. \qquad \text{III.c.23}$$

From (III.c.21 and 22) we obtain

$$-\frac{\bar{p}}{\bar{x}}\frac{d\bar{x}}{d\bar{p}} \equiv \bar{\eta} = 1 + \frac{1}{2\mu D} \qquad \text{III.c.24}$$

so that $\bar{\eta}/(\bar{\eta}-1) = 1 + \bar{\pi} = 1 + 2\mu D$, where $\bar{\eta}$ represents the expected elasticity of demand for the new firm's product and $2\mu D = \bar{\pi}$ represents its corresponding optimal price mark–up.

We will represent a firm's expected profit as

$$\bar{q}_k = \zeta_1 \bar{x}\bar{p} - \zeta_2 w\bar{l} - \zeta_3 h''\bar{k}. \qquad \text{III.c.25}$$

We introduce the parameters ζ_1, ζ_2 and ζ_3 in order to cover different institutional arrangements for the payment of the factors of production which we will discuss in Chapter V. In the Capitalist Wage Economy under discussion in the present chapter $\zeta_1 = \zeta_2 = \zeta_3 = 1$; in Chapter V these parameters will have other constant values.

Differentiation of (III.c.25) gives

$$d\bar{q}_k = \left(\zeta_1 \frac{\bar{x}\bar{p}}{\bar{k}}\frac{\alpha}{1+\bar{\pi}} - \zeta_3 h''\right) d\bar{k} + \left(\zeta_1 \frac{\bar{x}\bar{p}}{\bar{l}}\frac{\beta}{1+\bar{\pi}} - \zeta_2 w\right) d\bar{l} \qquad \text{III.c.26}$$

so that for the maximization of profit we will have

$$\bar{k} = \frac{\zeta_1}{\zeta_3}\frac{\bar{x}\bar{p}}{h''}\frac{\alpha}{1+\bar{\pi}} \text{ and } \bar{l} = \frac{\zeta_1}{\zeta_2}\frac{\bar{x}\bar{p}}{w}\frac{\beta}{1+\bar{\pi}}. \qquad \text{III.c.27}$$

From (III.c.27), with $xp = Y/m$, we can derive

$$x = \left(\frac{\zeta_1}{\zeta_3}\frac{Y}{mh''}\frac{\alpha}{1+\pi}\right)^{\alpha}\left(\frac{\zeta_1}{\zeta_2}\frac{Y}{mw}\frac{\beta}{1+\pi}\right)^{\beta} \qquad \text{III.c.28}$$

for the existing equilibrium outputs of the old firms.

For the new firm, using (III.c.22) for the value of $\bar{x}\bar{p}$ and (III.c.24) for the value of $1+\bar{\pi}$, we have

$$\bar{x} = \left(\frac{\zeta_1}{\zeta_3}\frac{2DY}{Hh''}\frac{\alpha}{1+2\mu D}\right)^{\alpha}\left(\frac{\zeta_1}{\zeta_2}\frac{2DY}{Hw}\frac{\beta}{1+2\mu D}\right)^{\beta}. \qquad \text{III.c.29}$$

From (III.c.28 and 29) we have

$$\frac{x}{\bar{x}} = \left(\frac{H}{2mD}\frac{1+2\mu D}{1+\pi}\right)^{1+\gamma} \qquad \text{III.c.30}$$

and with $xp = Y/m$, $\pi = \mu H/m$ and $\bar{x}\bar{p} = 2DY/H$ from (III.c.22) we can derive

$$\frac{\bar{p}}{p} = \frac{2mD}{H}\frac{x}{\bar{x}} = \left(\frac{\pi}{2\mu D}\right)^{\gamma}\left(\frac{1+2\mu D}{1+\pi}\right)^{1+\gamma}. \qquad \text{III.c.31}$$

From (III.c.20 and 31) we obtain

$$\left(\frac{\pi}{2\mu D}\right)^{\gamma} = \left(\frac{1+\pi}{1+2\mu D}\right)^{1+\gamma} e^{(\pi/2-2\mu D)} \qquad \text{III.c.32}$$

where $\gamma = \alpha + \beta - 1$ and $\pi = \mu H/m$. This expression determines the market span of the new firm ($2D$) in terms of the mark–up of the existing firms (π) and so in terms of the number of existing firms, since $m = \mu H/\pi$.

From (III.c.32) we obtain

$$\frac{dD}{D} = \frac{d\pi}{\pi}\frac{(\pi-\gamma)/(1+\pi)+\pi/2}{(2\mu D-\gamma)/(1+2\mu D)}. \qquad \text{III.c.33}$$

We are interested only in the cases in which $\pi \geqslant \gamma$ (since otherwise the existing firms would not survive because they would be making a loss as indicated in (III.b.16). From (III.c.24, 25 and 27) we can deduce that

$$\bar{q}_k = \zeta_1\bar{x}\bar{p}\,\frac{2\mu D-\gamma}{1+2\mu D}. \qquad \text{III.c.34}$$

It follows that if $2\mu D > \gamma$, $\bar{q}_k$ will be >0 and new firms will be attracted to enter. But π will be reduced by the entry of new firms and from (III.c.33) it follows that D will fall so that $2\mu D$ will be reduced towards γ. Indeed we may conclude that firms will enter the economy until $2\mu D = \gamma$.

If we substitute γ for $2\mu D$ in (III.c.32), we obtain

$$(1+\pi)\left(\frac{1+\pi}{\pi}\right)^{\gamma} e^{\pi/2} = (1+\gamma)\left(\frac{1+\gamma}{\gamma}\right)^{\gamma} e^{\gamma},$$

which, given the increasing–returns–to–scale factor III.c.35γ, determines the current profit mark–up factor π and so the current existing number of firms ($m = \mu H/\pi$) which will be just sufficient to discourage the entry of any more new firms.

If $\pi = \gamma$, i.e. if m were at the value $\bar{m}$ at which $q = 0$, then the LHS of (III.c.35) would be less than the RHS. But with $\pi \geqslant \gamma$ (and we can rule out the possibility of existing firms surviving at a loss) differentiation of the LHS of (III.c.35) shows that it increases with an increase in π, i.e. with a decrease in m. The number of firms at which equation (III.c.35) is solved will, therefore, be less than the number required to reduce q to zero and q will in consequence remain at a positive figure. A numerical example may help.

Suppose $\gamma = .1$. Then the solution of (III.c.35) would give $\pi \simeq .17$, so that the number of firms would be $m \simeq \mu H/.17 = 5.88\ \mu H$, whereas if firms were attracted so long as the existing firms were making any profit $\bar{\pi}$ would be reduced to .1 and the number of firms would rise to $\bar{m} = \mu H/.1 = 10\ \mu H$.

Note to Section (c) of Chapter III on a Geometrical Illustration of the Equilibrium Relationships between π and γ

In Figure III.c.2 we show the familiar micro relationship between the average and marginal curves for revenue and for cost in an imperfectly competitive market for a firm's product which is produced in conditions of increasing returns to scale. The average–revenue or demand–price curve (AR) is drawn with a constant price elasticity of demand of $\eta = 2$ which (see II.a.9) implies that the ratio of the average to the marginal revenue curve ($AR/MR = \eta/(\eta - 1) = 1 + \pi$) has a value of 2, and that with $\eta = 2$ we have a mark–up of average on marginal revenue of $\pi = 100$ per cent.

On the same figure we have drawn an average cost curve with a corresponding elasticity of 4, which (see II.c.13) gives a value of $1.\dot{3}$

for the ratio of average cost to marginal cost (AC/MC $= \eta/(\eta - 1) = 1 + \gamma$), so that the mark–up of AC on MC is $\gamma = 0.\dot{3}$.

As drawn in Figure III.c.2, the firm's output will be equal to o*a*, since with $x <$ o*a* MR is above MC and with $x >$ o*a* MR is below MC. Price will be equal to *ab*; cost per unit will be equal to *ac*; and total profit will be equal to *cbde*. It can be seen from the figure that, with constant elasticities, the existence of a determinate equilibrium with a positive finite output depends upon the assumption that the elasticity of demand is less than the elasticity of supply, i.e. that the price mark–up π is greater than the cost mark–up γ.

Suppose that the two elasticities were the same so that $\pi = \gamma$. Then the AR curve would be parallel to the AC curve and the MR curve parallel to the MC curve. If the demand curve were above the cost curve, the firm's output would expand indefinitely; if the demand curve were below the cost curve, output would fall to zero; if the two curves were the same height, any output could be produced so as just to cover costs. The position would be just as in conditions of constant returns to scale with perfect competition in which the single firm cannot affect the prices of its products or of its factors; there would be indefinite expansion if demand price exceeded cost per unit or indefinite contraction if demand price was below cost per unit. The reason for the analogy is clear. If $\pi = \gamma$, when the firm expands its output and sales, both cost per unit and selling price fall by the same percentage. Just as in the perfect–competition constant–cost case, the relationship between selling price and cost is unaffected.

Suppose then that we did start with AR > AC and $\pi = \gamma$. The firm's output will expand because in these conditions MR > MC. But in the real world expansion will not be infinite. At some point the elasticity of demand will fall (π will rise) because the market is swamped, or γ will fall because there is no further opportunity of taking advantage from large–scale production, or the cost of the factor inputs will be driven up because of the excessive demand by the firm for the factors of production.

In Figure III.c.3. we illustrate exactly the same cost conditions as in Figure III.c.2, but we consider the macro–economic constraints that are imposed by our present model on the micro–economic equilibrium. The micro–equilibrium position in Figure III.c.2 could already have illustrated the macro–equilibrium position if two conditions were fulfilled. In the first place, the area o*abd* in Figure III.c.2 must represent the total amount spent on the product of a single firm.

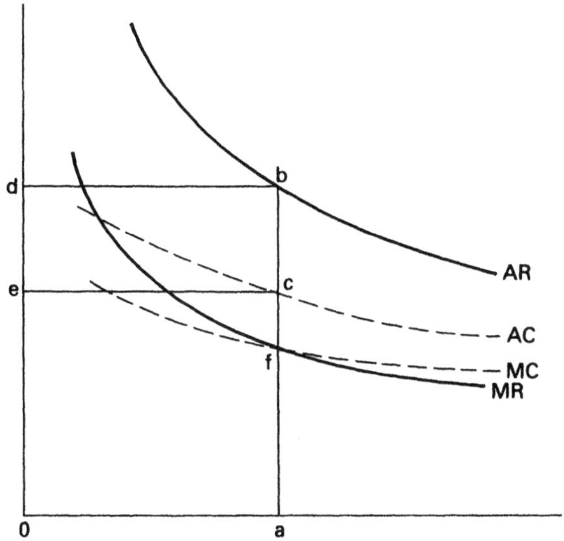

Figure III.c.2

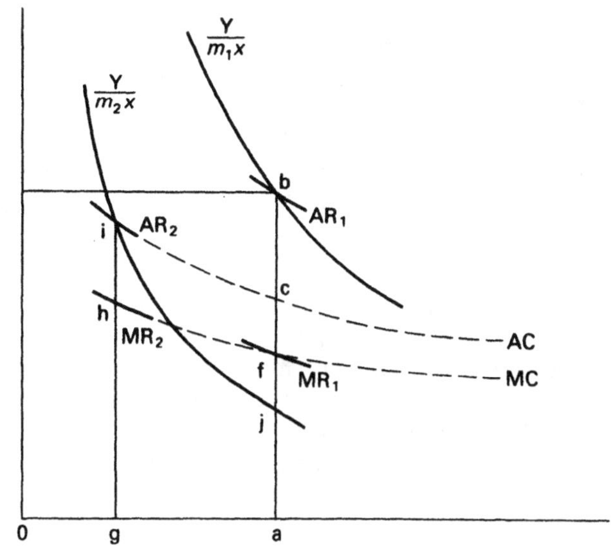

Figure III.c.3

This means that for the economy to be in equilibrium this area must be equal to the firm's *pro rata* share (Y/m) of the total money expenditure (Y) spread over the existing number of firms (m). The rectangular hyperbola curve marked Y/m_1x on Figure III.c.3 shows the relationship between the firm's selling price (p) and output (x) which will keep the firm's total revenue (xp) equal to Y/m when $m = m_1$. Equilibrium for the economy must lie on this curve. In the second place, equilibrium for the firm must be at a point on this curve at which the MR curve cuts the MC curve, so that the point b must lie not merely on the curve Y/mx but at a point on it which is $(1 + \pi)$ times the height of the MC curve.

In our macro–economic model the firm is not in fact faced by a constant–elasticity demand curve of a given height (as was assumed in the micro case of Figure III.c.2). The mark–up is based upon what the firm expects the elasticity of demand for its product to be if it were to increase its sales; and in our model (with $\pi = 2\mu D$ as in II.a.9) the expected elasticity will decrease and so π will increase with every increase in the firm's span over the market ($2D$). This span will increase (1) with a reduction in the number of firms, m, and thus with an increase in the firm's *pro rata* span of the market, or (2) with an invasion by the firm in question into the *pro rata* market spans of its neighbouring competitors.

If the economy is in equilibrium (i.e. with $xp = Y/m$ for every firm) and the number of firms is m_1, then the firm will be expecting an elasticity of demand which gives a mark-up of $\pi = \mu H/m_1$ (see II.a.10). This means that on every point on the curve Y/m_1x the expected elasticity of demand and so the relevant mark-up, $\pi = \mu H/m_1$, will remain constant. Simultaneous equilibrium for the firm and the economy can thus be found in Figure III.c.3 by finding a point b on the curve Y/m_1x such that the height of the curve MC is equal to $1/(1 + \pi)$ times the height of the curve Y/m_1x, where $\pi = \mu H/m_1$. At this point the expected MR will be $1/(1 + \pi)$ times AR and will be equal to the marginal cost MC.

Suppose now that with $\pi > \gamma$ more firms are attracted into production. As m increases two things will happen: first, the curve $p = Y/mx$ will fall and, second, the mark–up $\pi = \mu H/m$ will also fall. Let p_1 and π_1 represent the existing price and mark-up and let p_2 and π_2 represent the lower price and mark–up resulting from the increased number of firms. From the expressions $p = Y/mx$ and $\pi = \mu H/m$ we see that if x were constant we would have $p_1/p_2 = \pi_1/\pi_2 = m_2/m_1$. But we also have

$MR_1 = p_1/(1 + \pi_1)$ and $MR_2 = p_2/(1 + \pi_2)$, so that with x constant we would have $MR_2/MR_1 = \pi_2(1 + \pi_1)/\pi_1(1 + \pi_2)$. With $m_2 > m_1$, we have $\pi_1 > \pi_2$, so that $MR_2 < MR_1$. In other words, an increase in m with x constant would cause the expected marginal revenue of the firm to fall, so that with an unchanged marginal–cost curve the firm will reduce its output.

If firms go on entering until π is reduced to γ, we will end up with the position shown at points g, h and i on Figure III.c.3. The number of firms will fall until the price mark-up π falls to equality with γ, which means that the number of firms must increase from $m_1 = \mu H/\pi$ to $m_2 = \mu H/\gamma$, so that $m_1/m_2 = \gamma/\pi$. If x were constant we would then have $p_1 = Y/m_1x$ and $p_2 = Y/m_2x$ so that $p_2/p_1 = m_1/m_2 = \gamma/\pi$. But we have $AC = (1 + \gamma)MC$ and $p_1 = (1 + \pi)MR_1 = (1 + \pi)MC$ so that $AC = ([1 + \gamma]/[1 + \pi])p_1 = (\pi[1 + \gamma]/\gamma[1 + \bar{\pi}]\bar{p}_2$. Thus with $\gamma < \pi$ we have $p_2 < AC$.

This is illustrated in Figure III.c.3 which is drawn with $\gamma = 0.3$ and $\pi = 1$. With $p_2 = (\gamma[1 + \pi]/\pi[1 + \gamma])AC$, this implies $p_2 = 0.5AC$. Thus if x remained unchanged at its existing level of $x = oa$, the new Y/m_2x curve would have a height aj which was equal to 0.5 of the height of the AC curve, ac. The new equilibrium will be at the point i where the lower Y/m_2x curve cuts the old AC curve. At this point the firm's new expected demand curve will coincide with the average–cost curve, since (1) profit will be zero so that AC will equal AR, and (2) π will equal γ so that MC will equal MR.

With the AC and AR curves coinciding it might at first sight appear that the individual firm's output would be indeterminate, as in the case discussed above for the micro analysis of Figure III.c.2. But this is not the case. The two curves will coincide only at the point i. If the single firm increased its output, it would be invading its competitors' markets; and the consequential increase in its market span ($2D$) would cause its expected elasticity of demand to fall, so that its expected MR would fall below its MC. It would have an incentive to contract back again on to the macro equilibrium point i.

Figure III.c.3 can also be used to illustrate the effect of an increase in Y, the total money demand in the market as a whole. If each firm kept to its unchanged *pro rata* equilibrium span of the market, its expected price elasticity and thus its price mark-up π would remain unchanged. The curve Y/mx would shift upwards and to the right. With $\pi > \gamma$, the point f would move to the right along the MC curve until a new point b was found on the higher Y/m_1x curve which once more equated ab with $(1 + \pi)af$. With $\pi = \gamma$, the curve Y/m_2x would move upwards and to the right and a new equilibrium would be found where this higher Y/m_2x curve cut the AC curve. In both cases there would be an increase in the firm's output, x.

Throughout this geometrical note it has been assumed that the prices of the factors (w and h) remain unchanged. This will not be so if there is already full employment of a given factor (and throughout the main text it is assumed that there is always full employment of capital). In so far as factors are fully employed, an increase in demand would, as shown in the main text, cause a rise in the cost curve and so in selling price rather than in output.

(d) The Full–Employment Capitalist Wage Economy with a Given Number of Firms

In Sections (b) and (c) of this Chapter we assumed that the money wage rate was set exogenously at a level which was sufficiently high, given the level of total money expenditures, to restrict the demand for labour below the full employment level ($L < L^*$). In this section we consider the case in which there is full employment. This may come about because there is a competitive labour market in which the money wage rate is bid down (or up) until at that wage the demand for labour is exactly equal to the full–employment supply L^*. From (III.b.15) it can be seen that this implies a full–employment wage rate of

$$w^* = \frac{Y}{L^*}\frac{\beta}{1+\pi}. \qquad \text{III.d.1}$$

In conditions of full employment, equations (III.b.1 to 24) can be replaced by equations (III.d.2 to 25).

From equations (III.d.18 to 25) we see that in the full–employment situation a change in Y has no effect upon any of the real variables k, l, x, K, L or X but only on the money variables p, h, w, and q. An increase in m will reduce k and l (III.d.18 and 19) because it spreads the fixed total amounts of K^* and L^* over a larger number of firms; it will reduce total output (III.d.24) by the increasing–returns–to–scale factor γ because of the smaller scale of production in each firm; and it will reduce the output of each firm (III.d.19) both

$$xp = \frac{Y}{m} \qquad \text{III.d.2}$$

$$x = k^{\alpha} l^{\beta} \qquad 3$$

$$k = \frac{K^*}{m} \qquad 4$$

$$l = \frac{L^*}{m} \qquad 5$$

$$h = \frac{xp}{k} \frac{\alpha}{1+\pi} \qquad 6$$

$$w^* = \frac{Y}{L^*} \frac{\beta}{1+\pi} \qquad 7$$

$$X = mx \qquad 8$$

$$q = xp - wl - hk \qquad 9$$

Equations III.d.2 to 9

$$k = \frac{K^*}{m} \qquad \text{III.d.10}$$

$$l = \frac{L^*}{m} \qquad 11$$

$$x = \left(\frac{K^*}{m}\right)^{\alpha} \left(\frac{L^*}{m}\right)^{\beta} \qquad 12$$

$$p = \frac{Y}{m} \left(\frac{K^*}{m}\right)^{-\alpha} \left(\frac{L^*}{m}\right)^{-\beta} \qquad 13$$

$$h = \frac{Y}{K^*} \frac{\alpha}{1+\pi} \qquad 14$$

$$w^* = \frac{Y}{L^*} \frac{\beta}{1+\pi} \qquad 15$$

$$X = m^{-\gamma} (K^*)^{\alpha} (L^*)^{\beta} \qquad 16$$

$$q = \frac{Y}{m} \frac{\pi - \gamma}{1+\pi} \qquad 17$$

Equations III.d.10 to 17

$$\frac{\mathrm{d}k}{k} = -\frac{\mathrm{d}m}{m}$$ III.d.18

$$\frac{\mathrm{d}l}{l} = -\frac{\mathrm{d}m}{m}$$ 19

$$\frac{\mathrm{d}x}{x} = -(1+\gamma)\frac{\mathrm{d}m}{m}$$ 20

$$\frac{\mathrm{d}p}{p} = \frac{\mathrm{d}Y}{Y} + \gamma\frac{\mathrm{d}m}{m}$$ 21

$$\frac{\mathrm{d}h}{h} = \frac{\mathrm{d}Y}{Y} + \frac{\pi}{1+\pi}\frac{\mathrm{d}m}{m}$$ 22

$$\frac{\mathrm{d}w^*}{w^*} = \frac{\mathrm{d}Y}{Y} + \frac{\pi}{1+\pi}\frac{\mathrm{d}m}{m}$$ 23

$$\frac{\mathrm{d}X}{X} = -\gamma\frac{\mathrm{d}m}{m}$$ 24

$$\frac{\mathrm{d}q}{Y/m} = \frac{\pi-\gamma}{1+\pi}\left(\frac{\mathrm{d}Y}{Y} - \frac{\mathrm{d}m}{m}\right) - \frac{\pi(1+\gamma)}{(1+\pi)^2}\frac{\mathrm{d}w}{m}$$ 25

Equations III.d.18 to 25

by loss of increasing–returns–to–scale ($\gamma\ \mathrm{d}m/m$) and so of output per unit of input and also by the spread of the factor–inputs over a larger number of firms ($\mathrm{d}m/m$).

If we now consider the output of the economy after deduction of transport costs (namely $\hat{X} = \rho X$), we can write

$$\frac{\mathrm{d}\hat{X}}{\hat{X}} = \frac{\mathrm{d}X}{X} + \frac{\mathrm{d}\rho}{\rho}$$

which from (II.b.3) and (III.d.24) can be written as

$$\frac{\mathrm{d}\hat{X}}{\hat{X}} = \left(\frac{\pi}{4+\pi} - \gamma\right)\frac{\mathrm{d}m}{m}.$$ III.d.26

With $\pi = \mu H/m$ it can be seen from (III.d.26) that $\hat{X}$ will increase with an increase in m so long as $m < \mu H(1-\gamma)/4\gamma$. If we regard the maximization of $\hat{X}$ as the welfare objective, we can say that the optimum number of firms in a full–employment economy is given by

$$\hat{m} = \frac{\mu H(1-\gamma)}{4\gamma}. \qquad \text{III.d.27}$$

Since we are assuming that $2 > \alpha + \beta > 1$ (see II.c.1), it follows that $1 > \alpha + \beta - 1 > 0$. Thus, with the value of γ lying between 0 and 1, (III.d.27) shows that there will be a positive finite number of firms in the optimum situation and that this number ($\hat{m}$) will be the smaller, the greater is the increasing–returns–to–scale factor (γ).

(e) The Full–Employment Capitalist Wage Economy with a Market–Determined Number of Firms

We now assume as in Section (c) that firms enter the market until $q = 0$, so that from (III.c.2 and 3), $\bar{\pi} = \gamma$ and $\bar{m} = \mu H/\gamma$, a constant value which does not depend upon Y or w. Using these values of $\bar{\pi}$ and $\bar{m}$ and with $dm/m = 0$ we can rewrite equations (III.d.10 to 25) as in equations (III.e.1 to 16).

$$k = \frac{\gamma}{\mu H} K^* \qquad \text{III.e.1}$$

$$l = \frac{\gamma}{\mu H} L^* \qquad 2$$

$$x = \left(\frac{\gamma}{\mu H}\right)^{1+\gamma} (K^*)^{\alpha} (L^*)^{\beta} \qquad 3$$

$$p = Y\left(\frac{\gamma}{\mu H}\right)^{-\gamma} (K^*)^{-\alpha} (L^*)^{-\beta} \qquad 4$$

$$h = \frac{Y}{K^*} \frac{\alpha}{1+\gamma} \qquad 5$$

$$w^* = \frac{Y}{L^*} \frac{\beta}{1+\gamma} \qquad 6$$

$$X = \left(\frac{\gamma}{\mu H}\right)^{\gamma} (K^*)^{\alpha} (L^*)^{\beta} \qquad 7$$

$$q = 0 \qquad 8$$

Equations III.e.1 to 8

$$\frac{dk}{k} = 0 \qquad \text{III.e.9}$$

$$\frac{dl}{l} = 0 \qquad 10$$

$$\frac{dx}{x} = 0 \qquad 11$$

$$\frac{dp}{p} = \frac{dY}{Y} \qquad 12$$

$$\frac{dh}{h} = \frac{dY}{Y} \qquad 13$$

$$\frac{dw^*}{w^*} = \frac{dY}{Y} \qquad 14$$

$$\frac{dX}{X} = 0 \qquad 15$$

$$\frac{dq}{Y/m} = 0 \qquad 16$$

Equations III.e.9 to 16

Thus changes in Y have no effect on any of the real quantities which remain set at their full–employment levels; Y affects only the monetary values p, h, and w^* with q held by the entry of new firms at its zero level.

We can now make a most important and significant comparison. From (III.d.27) we deduced that in a full–employment equilibrium the optimum number of firms (i.e. the number which will give the best balance between concentration of output in order to take advantage of economies of scale and dispersion in order to increase variety of quality or to save transport costs by variety of locality) will be

$$\hat{m} = \frac{\mu H(1-\gamma)}{4\gamma}. \qquad \text{III.e.17}$$

From (III.c.3) we deduced that the market equilibrium number of firms would be

$$\tilde{m} = \frac{\mu H}{\gamma} \qquad \text{III.e.18}$$

so that

$$\hat{m} = \frac{1-\gamma}{4}\,\tilde{m}. \qquad \text{III.e.19}$$

Thus in the full–employment economy with a flexible competitive wage, in the absence of setting–up costs and with $0 < \gamma < 1$ we would have

$$\hat{m} < \tfrac{1}{4}\tilde{m}.$$

Thus with the structure of the monopolistic–competitive economy as modelled in this book the number of firms resulting from *laissez-faire* in the absence of setting–up costs would be some four times greater than the number which would best serve to reduce costs, even after allowance is made for the extra transport costs (or loss of variety of choice) due to the concentration of production. It is only through the presence of setting–up costs or of fixed overhead costs of the type indicated in the footnote on page 19 (both of which factors we are neglecting) that the number of firms might be kept down nearer their optimum level.

CHAPTER IV

The Non–Discriminating Labour Co–operative

(a) The Nature of a Non–Discriminating Labour Co–operative

In Chapter III we discussed an institutional set–up for the firm in which all or some of the owners of the capital resources bore the risks of the enterprise, took the decisions about output, employment, and capital investment, and hired the workers at a money wage rate which was the same for all workers. We now reverse the roles of capitalists and workers and assume that some or all of the workers bear the risks, take the decisions, and hire the capital resources at a single market–determined rate of hire.

The analysis of the outcome in Chapter III would be applicable without any change at all if we made one additional assumption. In Chapter III we explained that the 'entrepreneurial' factors (capitalists) admitted new capital resources on a discriminating principle, in the sense that when new capital funds were raised (whether by the issue of ordinary shares or of fixed–interest debentures) the new capitalists were offered a return on their funds which corresponded to the outside market rate but did not include any share of any return over and above that rate which was being already enjoyed by the existing capitalist entrepreneurs. As a result the maximization of the profit of the already established entrepreneurs always implied taking on more capital so long as the outside market rate of hire was less than the marginal revenue product of the capital equipment.

The analogue to this in the case of a Labour Co–operative would be that the workers who were the established entrepreneurs at any one time would offer to new workers (whether in the form of a fixed money wage or in the forms of a share in the firm's net revenue after the payment of the capital costs) a reward which was equal to the outside market rate of payment for work and which did not include any of the 'profit' over and above that rate of pay which was being enjoyed by the already established worker–entrepreneurs. This would involve the discriminating principle that new workers might be working at the same bench with the old workers but at a lower rate of pay. If this principle were adopted, then – as in the case of the Capitalist Wage Economy discussed in Chapter III – decisions would be taken which aimed at maximizing q, the total profit over and above the market cost of the labour and capital equipment which was employed. The only difference would be that the resulting q would be distributed among some or all of the existing workers instead of being distributed among some or all of the existing capitalists.

We intend in this chapter to analyse the case in which this discriminating principle is not applied to the payment of the workers. The workers bear the risks, take the decisions, hire the capital at the ruling market rate of hire, but in all cases distribute the residual worker–income on a non–discriminating principle equally among all workers.

In Chapter III the firm's maximand was the total capitalists' profit

$$\bar{q}_k = \bar{x}\bar{p} - h\bar{k} - w\bar{l}$$

as in (III. a.1).

In this chapter the firm's maximand is the profit per head of the workers in employment in the co–operative, which in the notation outlined in the note at the end of Chapter I is given by the expression

$$q_l/l = w' - w'' = \frac{xp - h'k}{l} - w''.$$

With $h' = h'' = h$, that is to say, with the co–operative workers hiring all their capital at a fixed rent (h) equal to the outside market rate (h'') and with w'' constant at the outside opportunity pay of the workers, we may express the maximand for the Non–Discriminating Labour Co–operative as

$$\bar{w}' = \frac{\bar{x}\bar{p} - h\bar{k}}{\bar{l}} \qquad \text{IV.a.1}$$

which measures the earnings per head of the workers in employment in the co–operative.

Differentiation of (IV.a.1), using (II.a.9) for the market conditions in which $\bar{x}$ is sold at price $\bar{p}$ and using (II.c.1, 2 and 3) for the way in which $\bar{k}$ and $\bar{l}$ produce $\bar{x}$, gives

$$d\bar{w}' = \frac{1}{\bar{l}}\left\{\left(\frac{\bar{x}\bar{p}}{\bar{k}}\frac{\alpha}{1+\bar{\pi}} - h\right) d\bar{k} + \left(\frac{\bar{x}\bar{p}}{\bar{l}}\frac{\beta}{1+\bar{\pi}} - \bar{w}'\right)\right\}. \qquad \text{IV.a.2}$$

From (IV.a.2) it follows that $\bar{k}$ will be employed up to the point at which

$$\frac{\bar{x}\bar{p}}{\bar{k}}\frac{\alpha}{1+\bar{\pi}} = h \qquad \text{IV.a.3}$$

and the number of partner–workers will be increased or decreased according as

$$\frac{\bar{x}\bar{p}}{\bar{l}}\frac{\beta}{1+\bar{\pi}} \gtrless \bar{w}'. \qquad \text{IV.a.4}$$

(IV.a.3 and 4) express the familiar conclusion of the Labour Co–operative organization, namely that, as in the Capitalist Wage Economy, capital will be employed up to the point at which the cost of the capital is equal to its marginal revenue product, but that new worker partners will be taken on only up to the point at which the marginal revenue product of labour is equal to the existing average income per worker.

(b) The Instability of the Non-Discriminating Labour Co–operative Economy[1]

We now reach some surprising and uncomfortable conclusions about the way in which the Non–Discriminating Labour Co–operative Economy would behave on the assumption about market conditions made in Section (a) and about the production function made in Section (c) of Chapter II.

From (IV.a.3) it is clear that it will pay a firm to invest in capital resources in a way such that.the total capital cost ($h\bar{k}$) is equal to a given proportion ($\alpha/(1 + \bar{\pi})$) of the firm's revenue ($\bar{x}\bar{p}$). With a high cost of hire (h) little capital ($\bar{k}$) will be used and *vice versa*; but the

[1] For an earlier discussion of the instability of a labour co-operative, see J. E. Meade 'The adjustment processes of labour co-operatives with constant returns to scale and perfect competition', *Economic Journal* (December, 1979), pp. 781–8.

total capital cost will maintain its fixed ratio to total revenue. From (IV.a.4), substituting for $\bar{w}'$ and $h\bar{k}$ from (IV.a.1 and 3) we then reach the conclusion that it will pay the co-operative to take on more or less worker partners according as

$$\frac{\bar{x}\bar{p}}{\bar{l}}\frac{\beta}{1+\bar{\pi}} \gtrless \frac{\bar{x}\bar{p}}{\bar{l}}\left(1-\frac{\alpha}{1+\bar{\pi}}\right) \qquad \text{IV.b.1}$$

i.e. as $\gamma \gtrless \bar{\pi}$.

The *raison d'être* of this conclusion can be understood in the following way. As we have already explained, $\bar{\pi}$ measures the mark–up of price on marginal revenue and γ measures the mark–up of average cost on marginal cost; if marginal cost is equated with marginal revenue, there will be an excess of average cost over selling price (i.e. a loss instead of a profit) if $\gamma > \bar{\pi}$. The Labour Co–operative is one in which any such residual 'profit' or 'loss' is distributed evenly over the workers who, in fact, receive the residual after all other costs have been met. Thus, with capital receiving its marginal revenue product, we may regard the worker as receiving his or her marginal revenue product plus (or minus) a *pro rata* share of any structural profit (or loss) measured by the $\bar{q}_s = \bar{q} = \bar{x}\bar{p}(\bar{\pi} - \gamma)/(1 + \bar{\pi})$ of (III.b.16).

Suppose then that $\gamma > \bar{\pi}$, i.e. that there is a 'loss' in the sense that $\bar{q} < 0$. The average income of the worker will thus be lower than the worker's marginal revenue product by his share of the $\bar{q}$. But these are the conditions in which the co-operative has an incentive to take on more partners. A new worker will add his marginal revenue product $((\bar{x}\bar{p}/\bar{l})(\beta/[1 + \bar{\pi}]))$ to the total income available to the workers as a whole; but with $\gamma > \bar{\pi}$ this will be greater than the existing workers' average income, so that the new worker will contribute some surplus available to raise the existing workers' average income. In these conditions the existing partners will want to take on a new partner provided that the new partner is willing to join the co–operative at the existing income per partner. From (IV. a.3) with $\alpha/(1 + \pi) < 1$, it is clear that payments for the hire of capital will not absorb the whole of the co–operative's revenue, so that the remaining income per head in the partnership will be positive. If all co–operatives are in the same position and there are unemployed workers with zero incomes, the co–operatives will be able to attract new partners at their existing income per head.

Suppose that in these conditions one co–operative expands on the assumption that none of the other co–operatives are following suit; this process of expansion of the single co–operative will not continue indefinitely. From (II.a.9) we know that $\bar{\pi} = 2\mu D$ or, in other words, that as the co–operative increases its market span the expected elasticity of demand for its product will fall as indicated by a rise in its mark–up factor $\bar{\pi}$. This rise in $\bar{\pi}$ means that the marginal revenue product of labour will be reduced relatively to the average revenue product of labour (see the LHS of IV.b.1). At the same time, since from (IV.a.3) $h\bar{k}/\bar{x}\bar{p} = \alpha/(1 + \bar{\pi})$, the proportion of the average revenue product which is absorbed by capital costs will fall (see the RHS of IV.b.1). When $\bar{\pi}$ has risen to γ, the marginal revenue product of labour will have fallen to equality with the average income per worker and the co–operative's incentive to expand will cease.

But the outcome is quite different if all co–operatives together act in this way. Consider a starting point with m co–operatives spread evenly round the market circle each with a market span of $2D = H/m$. Suppose further that m is sufficiently large for $\pi = 2\mu D = \mu H/m$ to be $<\gamma$. Each co–operative will be making a 'loss' with average wage income less than labour's marginal revenue product. All the co–operatives will expand simultaneously. As they do so total output ($X = mx$) will rise; and with total money expenditure (Y) unchanged, selling prices (p) will fall. But the individual co–operative's market span (H/m) will not have changed and the expected elasticity of demand for its product and hence its profit mark–up ($\pi = \mu H/m$) will remain unchanged. There will be no rise in π to reduce the LHS relative to the RHS of (IV.b.1). The incentive to expand will persist indefinitely until expansion becomes impossible because all available workers have been absorbed into the Labour Co–operatives ($L = L^*$).

The whole of this analysis can be put into reverse if $\pi > \gamma$. In this case each co–operative starts with a 'profit', i.e. with the average worker income greater than its marginal revenue product. If one less partner were admitted the loss to total workers' income would be less than the average income so that the average income could be raised. If all co–operatives were behaving simultaneously in this contractionary way, output would be reduced and price would be raised, but the profit mark–up (π) would not be changed. Contraction of the scale of each co–operative would go on indefinitely.

The preceding analysis has been conducted on the assumption that there is an exogenously fixed number of co–operatives with the result that according as this given number was greater or less than the number needed to equate π to γ, so there would be indefinite expansion or contraction of employment and output. From (III.c.3) we can conclude that there will be indefinite contraction or expansion of output according as

$$m \lesseqgtr \bar{m} = \frac{\mu H}{\gamma}. \qquad \text{IV.b.2}$$

We will return later to the question what it is which determines the number of firms, m.

(c) Reconciliation with the Classical Analysis of Labour Co–operatives

The conclusions reached in Section (b) above may appear at first sight in conflict with the familiar conclusions reached about the behaviour of Labour Co–operatives. In particular the conclusion that if the number of competing co–operatives is sufficiently great, they will automatically expand the scale of their operations until there is full employment may seem to be in conflict with the familiar conclusions: (1) that there is a contractionary bias in Labour Co–operatives whose objective is to maximize 'profit' per head rather than total profit, and (2) that expansionary forces will exist only from an increase in the number of co–operatives based on the reliance on free entry of new co–operatives so long as there is any unemployment.

This apparent conflict of analysis can be explained in the following way. We are considering a co–operative which acts as if it were confronted with a demand curve with a price elasticity of $\bar{\eta} = 1 + 1/\bar{\pi}$ (see II.a.8 and 9). We can in this case write its demand curve as

$$\bar{x} = A\bar{p}^{-\bar{\eta}},$$

where A is a constant scale parameter, so that

$$\bar{x}\bar{p} = A^{1/\eta}\bar{x}^{(\bar{\eta}-1)/\bar{\eta}} = A^{\bar{\pi}/(1+\bar{\pi})}\bar{x}^{1/(1+\bar{\pi})}. \qquad \text{IV.c.1}$$

Suppose that this co-operative was burdened with an interest debt of $H = hk$ and that for some reason or another this capital cost position was fixed and unalterable. Then from (IV.a.1 and 4) we could conclude that the co–operative would have an incentive to expand the partnership until

$$\frac{\bar{x}\bar{p}}{1+\bar{\pi}}\frac{\beta}{\bar{l}}=\frac{\bar{x}\bar{p}-H}{\bar{l}},$$

that is to say, using (IV.c.1), until

$$\bar{x}\bar{p}=A^{\bar{\pi}/(1+\bar{\pi})}\bar{x}^{1/(1+\bar{\pi})}=\frac{1+\bar{\pi}}{1+\bar{\pi}-\beta}H. \qquad \text{IV.c.2}$$

From (IV.c.2) with $\bar{\pi}$ and β given it can be deduced that $\partial\bar{x}/\partial A<0$ and $\partial\bar{x}/\partial H>0$. These are the familiar perverse reactions of the Labour Co–operative for which an increase in demand will cause a reduction in output, and an increase in lump sum overhead costs will lead to an increase in output.

In the present model we are not holding H constant but, from (IV.a.3), are assuming that investment in capital will be increased so long as

$$H=h\bar{k}<\frac{\alpha}{1+\bar{\pi}}\bar{x}\bar{p}. \qquad \text{IV.c.3}$$

Consider then a co-operative with an existing overhead capital cost of H. In accordance with (IV.c.2) it will have an incentive to increase output and sales until $\bar{x}\bar{p}=([1+\bar{\pi}]/[1+\bar{\pi}-\beta])\,H$, i.e. until $H=([1+\bar{\pi}-\beta]/[1+\pi])\,\bar{x}\bar{p}$. Suppose that it does so. It will now reconsider its investment programme in the light of (IV.c.3). If $(1+\bar{\pi}-\beta)/(1+\bar{\pi})=\alpha/(1+\bar{\pi})$, then it will be content with its present capital investment. If, however, $(1+\bar{\pi}-\beta)/(1+\bar{\pi})<\alpha/(1+\bar{\pi})$, i.e. if $\bar{\pi}<\gamma$, it will have an incentive to expand its capital investment programme until $H=(\alpha/[1+\bar{\pi}])\,\bar{x}\bar{p}$. But with this increase in H, it will have an incentive to increase its output and sales until once more $\bar{x}\bar{p}$ has risen to $([1+\bar{\pi}]/[1+\bar{\pi}-\beta])H$. And so on, in an expansionary process which would not converge if $\bar{\pi}$ as well as α and β remained constant. Conversely, if $\bar{\pi}>\gamma$ there would be a process of restriction at work which would be non–convergent if $\bar{\pi}$ remained constant.[1]

[1] We may return again to a consideration of equation (IV.c.2) in the conditions in which we are dealing with the simultaneous expansion of all co–operatives. We could then write (IV.c.2) in the form of saying that each partnership would expand so long as

$$xp=\frac{Y}{m}<\frac{1+\pi}{1+\pi-\beta}H. \qquad \text{IV.c.4}$$

In brief, we may sum up the process in the following way. An expansion of the co–operative's partnership will be favourable if (1) the expected elasticity of demand for the co–operative's product is high so that not much is lost by the need to cut its selling price in order to expand its market and (2) there are important increasing returns to scale which can be enjoyed by an expansion of production and sales. Condition (1) will be fulfilled if the number of competing firms is large so that π is low, and condition (2) will be fulfilled if γ is high. With the assumed market conditions, production function, and macro behaviour which lead to a constant π and γ, these conditions will lead to a non–convergent expansion. Conversely with $\pi > \gamma$ there would be a non–convergent contraction.

As we saw in the discussion of (IV.c.2), the usual micro analysis of the Labour Co–operative states that the burden of a high overhead cost combined with a low level of demand will induce the co-operative to expand, whereas a low overhead cost combined with a high demand will tempt it to contract. It would seem that the Labour Co–operative relies upon the stick rather than the carrot to promote expansion. The macro analysis of the present chapter states that, in the parlance of a capitalist–wage enterprise, it is loss–making conditions which induce expansion and profit–making conditions which induce contraction; once again this suggests that it is the misery of the stick rather than the enjoyment of the carrot which activates the organization.

(d) Full–Employment in a Non–Discriminating Labour Co–operative Economy

If the number of firms m is $> \bar{m}$, the individual co–operatives will, on the basis of the analysis in the preceding chapter, expand until there is full employment. The resulting position can be expressed in

---

Comparing this with (IV.c.2), x, has a constant value, namely Y/m, π remains a constant at π because the number of firms is constant and each firm's market span remains unchanged, and H remains a constant *either because we are simply assuming there to be a fixed overhead constant charge,* or, as in our macro–economic model because we assume that investment decisions result in $H(=hK)$ being a constant proportion $\alpha/(1+\pi)$ of a constant revenue Y/m. Thus whether or not we are allowing for a change in investment decisions or are simply assuming a fixed money overhead capital charge, the macro implications of our model would lead to an indefinite expansion of each partnership if condition (IV.c.4) were satisfied.

equations (IV.d.1 to 21)

$$xp = \frac{Y}{m} \qquad \text{IV.d.1}$$

$$k = \frac{K^*}{m} \qquad 2$$

$$l = \frac{L^*}{m} \qquad 3$$

$$x = k^{\alpha} l^{\beta} \qquad 4$$

$$h = \frac{xp}{k} \frac{\alpha}{1+\pi} \qquad 5$$

$$X = mx \qquad 6$$

$$w' = \frac{xp - kh}{l} \qquad 7$$

Equations IV.d.1 to 7

These equations (IV.d.1 to 7) can be rearranged to give equations (IV.d.8 to 14).

$$k = \frac{K^*}{m} \qquad \text{IV.d.8}$$

$$l = \frac{L^*}{m} \qquad 9$$

$$x = \left(\frac{K^*}{m}\right)^{\alpha} \left(\frac{L^*}{m}\right)^{\beta} \qquad 10$$

$$p = \frac{Y}{m} \left(\frac{K^*}{m}\right)^{-\alpha} \left(\frac{L^*}{m}\right)^{-\beta} \qquad 11$$

$$h = \frac{Y}{K^*} \frac{\alpha}{1+\pi} \qquad 12$$

$$X = m^{-\gamma}(K^*)^{\alpha}(L^*)^{\beta} \qquad 13$$

$$w' = \frac{Y}{L^*}\frac{1+\pi-\alpha}{1+\pi} \qquad 14$$

Equations IV.d.8 to 14

From equations (IV.d.8 to 14) one can then derive equations (IV.d.15 to 21).

$$\frac{dk}{k} = -\frac{dm}{m} \qquad \text{IV.d.15}$$

$$\frac{dl}{l} = -\frac{dm}{m} \qquad 16$$

$$\frac{dx}{x} = -(1+\gamma)\frac{dm}{m} \qquad 17$$

$$\frac{dp}{p} = \frac{dY}{Y} + \gamma\frac{dm}{m} \qquad 18$$

$$\frac{dh}{h} = \frac{dY}{Y} + \frac{\pi}{1+\pi}\frac{dm}{m} \qquad 19$$

$$\frac{dX}{X} = -\gamma\frac{dm}{m} \qquad 20$$

$$\frac{dw'}{w'} = \frac{dY}{Y} - \frac{\pi}{1+\pi}\,\frac{a}{1+\pi-\alpha}\,\frac{dm}{m} \qquad 21$$

Equations IV.d.15 to 21

The results are exactly the same as in equations (III.d.2 to 25) for the Full–Employment Capitalist Wage Economy with a given number of firms except that we are now not interested in w^* (the full–employment wage rate) and q (the profit or loss) separately, but in the composite w' (the income of wage–cum–profit per head).

Equations (IV.d.15 to 21) show that, as in the case of equations (III.d.18 to 25), a change in Y will affect none of the real variables (k, l, x, and X) but only the monetary variables ($p, h,$ and w'). A change in m will have the same effect as in the Full–Employment Capitalist Wage Economy on $k, l, x, p, h,$ and X. The effect on w' of an increase in m will be on balance negative because the reward offered to attract capital, and so the hire charged for capital, will be raised as a result of the increased competition raising the marginal revenue product of capital. The share of the money national income which will go to the hire of capital equipment which from (IV.d.12) can be expressed as $hK^*/Y = \alpha/(1+\pi)$ will rise as m increases and π is reduced. As a result there will be some erosion of w'.

It is of interest to ask what will happen to the real income per worker, i.e. to $w'/\hat{p}$ where $\hat{p} = p/\rho$. From (II.b.3) and (IV.d.18 and 21) we obtain

$$\frac{\mathrm{d}(w'/\hat{p})}{w'/\hat{p}} = \frac{\mathrm{d}\rho}{\rho} + \frac{\mathrm{d}w'}{w'} - \frac{\mathrm{d}p}{p}$$

$$= \left(\frac{\pi}{4+\pi} - \frac{\pi}{1+\pi}\frac{\alpha}{1+\alpha} - \gamma\right)\frac{\mathrm{d}m}{m}. \qquad \text{IV.d.22}$$

An increase in m will raise the real income of the workers in so far as it reduces transport costs or increases the variety of products, but it will reduce it in so far as it increases the competition for capital resources causing a rise in the proportion of income going to the owners of capital and in so far as the cost of living is raised through a loss of output due to a reduction in the economies of large–scale production.

(e) Factors Affecting the Number of Co–operatives

We have argued that if $m > \bar{m}$, all the existing co–operatives will expand until there is full employment of labour and each co–operative is checked in its search for additional partners simply by the absence of any unemployment. We made the tacit assumption that every co–operative would have the same success in its efforts to expand so that each co–operative would end up at the same size, namely with L^*/m partners.

This situation is, however, potentially a very unstable one. Suppose one co-operative managed to get ahead of another so that co-operative 1 had $l_1 > L^*/m$ partners and co-operative 2 had $l_2 < L^*/m$ partners. Co-operative 1 would now have a higher w'_1 than co-operative 2's w'_2, because co-operative 1 would have gained and co-operative 2 would have lost workers whose marginal revenue product was greater than the average income. Workers would be tempted to leave co-operative 2 and join co-operative 1 which would still be seeking new partners, a process which might well take the form of a take-over of co-operative 2 by co-operative 1 and their combination into a single larger-scale co-operative. This process would be a grubby affair, since it would involve reductions in the number of co-operatives together with their replacing themselves at equal distances from each other around the market circle with larger market intervals between the reduced number of co-operatives. But in principle there is no reason why the reduction in the number of co-operatives should not continue until $m = \tilde{m}$.

If, on the other hand, $m < \tilde{m}$ in the original situation, then, as we have argued in Section (b), each co-operative would have an incentive to contract. As a result there would be a continuous growth in the number of unemployed workers. If we assume that any social-security-fiscal support for the unemployed was small relative to the w' which would be received in a co-operative and if we further make the heroic assumptions that the unemployed workers have the same managerial skills, enterprise, and ready access to the capital market as do the remaining employed workers in the existing co-operatives, new co-operatives will be set up by the unemployed workers. And the more the existing co-operatives reduce the size of their partnership, the greater the number of new partnerships that will be formed. There is no reason why this growth of numbers should not continue until $m = \tilde{m}$.

By these two processes of amalgamation of co-operatives if $m > \tilde{m}$ and setting up of new co-operatives if $m < \tilde{m}$, m may be kept more or less equal to $\tilde{m}$. But there would always be a potential instability of the size of existing co-operatives in the region of $m \simeq \tilde{m}$, an instability which would have to be kept in check by the ponderous, slow, and grubby process of change in the number of co-operatives and their dispersion at even intervals round the market circle.

In so far, however, as m was kept equal to $\tilde{m}$, the results would be exactly the same as those shown in Section (e) of Chapter III for the

Capitalist Wage Economy in Full Equilibrium by equations (III.e.1 to 16), with w' instead of $w^* = (Y/L^*)(\beta/[1+\gamma])$ and with neglect of $q = 0$. The average income of the workers would be equal to their marginal revenue product and the outcome would be the same in both types of business – apart, of course, from any psychological or other effects of the different structures upon workers' incentives and so upon the production function.

(f) Concluding Observations on the Non–Discriminating Labour Co–operative

The idea of Labour Co–operatives is clearly a most attractive one, particularly in so far as it might reduce the sense of alienation between 'workers' and 'bosses' by making the workers their own bosses and thereby improving industrial relations, raising incentives, and thus increasing output and productivity. But, alas, a number of problems crop up in such an institutional organization, as has been suggested in the preceding analysis in this chapter.

Thus it would appear that there is an unfortunate built–in element of instability in the structure of a system of Non-Discriminating Labour Co–operatives.

A necessary condition for this instability is the recognition in the payment of labour of what we have called the Non–Discriminating Principle. Consider a successful Labour Co–operative in which a substantial 'profit' is being made which in fact is being used to boost the income per head of the existing partners. It may well be that at the same time the marginal revenue product of a new worker is higher than what a worker can earn elsewhere and is high enough, therefore, to attract an additional partner. But if it is lower than the 'wage' plus 'profit' of the existing partners it will not be allowed to attract new partners because the new partner would in addition have to be paid his or her share of the existing 'profit'. The higher the existing 'profit', the greater the incentive to restrict output and employment. This is a perversity which could be countered by the acceptance of a certain degree of discrimination as will be suggested in Chapter VI below.

To offset this perversity, success with Non–Discriminating Labour Co–operatives depends, very much more than in a system of Capitalist Wage Firms, upon ease of entry and exit of new businesses. If a Capitalist Wage Firm is making a high profit it may not expand as much as one could wish; but unlike a 'profitable' Non–Discriminating Labour Co–operative it will not have a built–in and perhaps explosive incentive to contract its operations, which can be countered only by the fact that there will be an incentive to set up new competing co–operatives. But in the real world of risks, imperfect capital markets, and of scarcity of entrepreneurial initiatives entry into a market by new co–operatives may be far from easy.

Furthermore the offsetting of the innate contractionary forces in a system of Non–Discriminating Labour Co–operatives rests upon the number of co–operatives rising to a level equal to, or greater than, $\tilde{\bar{m}} = \mu H/\gamma$. But, as has been argued in Section (e) of Chapter III (see III.e.19), $\tilde{\bar{m}}$ would itself be more than four times the optimal number of firms in a full–employment economy in the absence of setting–up costs. Thus it would seem that a full–employment Labour Co–operative economy would exist only with a number of co–operatives which, while large enough to cause sufficient competition to induce expansion, could be much in excess of the number which would make the best of the balance between increasing returns to scale and variety of quality or location of the product. It might be possible in a Capitalist Wage Economy to take measures to prevent the growth in the number of 'profitable' concerns far beyond the optimum number and yet to promote the expansion of those firms to provide full employment. But it might be difficult in a Non–Discriminating Labour Co–operative system to take measures to restrict the number of 'profitable' co–operatives without giving the existing 'profitable' concerns an incentive to contract their employment.

There remains a number of awkward questions about Labour Co–operatives which arise in the real world, but which are not in fact raised by the formal, simple, precise models constructed in this book: for example, in any line of industry in which very capital–intensive techniques of production are essential, the workers would bear an intolerable degree of risk if any fluctuation in revenue fell upon their 'wage' after deduction of the very large overhead capital costs which would exist if the whole of the capital equipment had been financed by the issue of fixed–interest debt; and it would no longer be a straightforward labour co–operative if those who provided the capital funds shared the risks and took part, therefore, in decisions about investment, product, sales, and employment. Moreover, there is the question whether the owners of the capital funds would have the required degree of confidence in a large number of Labour Co–operatives or, in other words, whether the ease of access to the capital market of groups of workers who did not own much capital would be sufficient to make the system work successfully. One particular aspect of this problem of access to capital funds would be how to control and determine ownership of any capital developments which were financed by the ploughing back into the co–operative of some of its own 'profit' or revenue.

In Chapter VI an attempt will be made to outline the principles upon which a partnership system might be constructed which avoided some of the difficulties and problems encountered in the present chapter without sacrificing the central ideas of participation both in decision–making and in sharing of the rewards of effort, which lie at the root of the co–operative idea.

CHAPTER V

The Capitalist Sharing Economy

(a) Two Forms of the Capitalist Sharing Economy

By a Capitalist Sharing firm we mean one in which some or all of the owners of the capital, either directly or through representative managers, take the decisions about output, prices, employment and investment; but in which some or all of the workers receive a part or the whole of their pay in the form of an agreed share of part or the whole of the value added of the firm.

The fund of which the workers receive a contractual share may take either of two forms. In what we will call the Capitalist Revenue–Sharing firm the inclusive rate of pay of the worker can be expressed as

$$w' = w + \frac{sxp}{l}, \qquad \text{V.a.1}$$

where w' is the worker's inclusive rate of pay and w is the fixed wage element in his pay, which is supplemented by a proportion, s, of the total revenue of the firm, xp, distributed between the workers, l.

The profit of the capitalist entrepreneurs can then be expressed as

$$\left.\begin{aligned} q_K &= xp - w'l - h''k \\ &= (1-s)xp - wl - h''k \end{aligned}\right\} \qquad \text{V.a.2}$$

where h'' measures the outside market hire–charge for a unit of capital so that $h''k$ represents the total cost of employing the firm's capital equipment, a cost which takes the form either of a direct payment of interest on borrowed funds or the cost to the capitalist entrepreneurs due the the lost opportunity of earning interest in the market on the funds which they have instead risked in their business.

This is not the only possible form of share–economy arrangement. The arrangement may be to pay to the workers a share, s, of what we may call the 'accounting profit' of the firm. In this case q_a measures the accounting profit where

$$q_a = xp - wl - hk, \qquad \text{V.a.3}$$

where w is the fixed–wage element in the worker's pay and h is the fixed–interest element in the return to the capitalists.

The profit of the capitalist entrepreneurs is then

$$\left.\begin{aligned} q_K &= (1-s)(xp - wl - hk) + hk - h''k \\ &= (1-s)(xp - wl) - (h'' - sh)k. \end{aligned}\right\} \qquad \text{V.a.4}$$

They receive $(1-s)q_a$ as their share of the accounting profit plus the fixed interest paid to them (hk), but from this they must deduct the outside market hire–charge for their capital funds ($h''k$). We will call this a Capitalist Profit–Sharing firm.

The difference in principle between the two forms of sharing arrangement is as follows. In the revenue–sharing firm the workers are paid their fixed wage and a share of the whole revenue. In the profit–sharing arrangement the workers are paid their fixed wage *and the capitalists their fixed rate of return on the capital*, and the workers then receive their share of the remainder of the firm's revenue. As will be shown in what follows, these two different principles can lead to very different results.

It is interesting to note the extreme or pure forms of these two different arrangements. The pure revenue–sharing arrangement is one in which there are no fixed–wage or fixed–interest payments ($w = h = 0$), all incomes taking the form of a share of the revenue. In this case (V.a.2) becomes

$$q_K = (1-s)xp - h''k. \qquad \text{V.a.5}$$

It may be noted that the profit–sharing arrangement of (V.a.4) approaches the more nearly to this same result, the smaller are the fixed–pay elements w and h.

The pure profit–sharing arrangement may, however, best be defined as that in which the fixed–pay elements are set at the full market charges for the factors, (i.e. $w = w''$ and $h = h''$) in which case (V.a.4) becomes

$$q_K = (1-s)(xp - w''l - h''k). \qquad \text{V.a.6}$$

Labour and capital receive their full market costs in a fixed–payment form and simply share between them any pure profit or pure loss which remain.

(b) The Capitalist Sharing Economy with Rigid Pay Parameters and Unemployment

We will start our analysis of sharing arrangements with the assumption that the two pay parameters, namely the workers' share (s) and the fixed wage (w), are both rigidly fixed by an outside agency (e.g. a rigid national wage bargain or even by government edict.) Similarly, we start with the assumption that the fixed–interest element in the return on capital (h) is rigidly fixed. Whether or not this corresponds to any realistic situation it enables us to analyse some basic relationships which may remain important in so far as these parameters are slow and sticky in their adjustments.

In the case of a revenue–sharing firm with s, w and h'' constant differentiation of the value for an individual firm of its $\bar{q}_k$ given by the second expression for q_k in (V.a.2) results in

$$d\bar{q}_k = \{(1+s)x - h''\}\, d\bar{k} + \{(1-s)\lambda - w\}\, d\bar{l}, \qquad \text{V.b.1}$$

where, from (II.c.15), $x = (\bar{x}\bar{p}/\bar{k})(\alpha/[1+\bar{\pi}])$ measures the marginal revenue product of capital and $\lambda = (\bar{x}\bar{p}/\bar{l})(\beta/[1+\bar{\pi}])$ measures the marginal revenue product of labour.

The individual firm will thus have an incentive to invest in more capital so long as

$$\bar{k} < \frac{\bar{x}\bar{p}}{h''} \cdot \frac{\alpha(1-s)}{1+\bar{\pi}} \qquad \text{V.b.2}$$

and to employ more labour so long as

$$\bar{l} < \frac{\bar{x}\bar{p}}{w} \cdot \frac{\beta(1-s)}{1+\bar{\pi}}. \qquad \text{V.b.3}$$

We are assuming throughout that the authorities set a hire–charge for capital which results in the employment of K^* units of capital in equilibrium. This means that each firm employs its *pro rata* share

K^*/m, and receives its *pro rata* share of total revenue Y/m. From (V.b.2) we thus derive the value of h'' which must be set by the authorities to obtain this result, namely

$$h'' = (1-s)x = (1-s)\frac{Y}{K^*}\frac{\alpha}{1+\pi}. \qquad \text{V.b.4}$$

But with w and s arbitrarily fixed and with each firm receiving its *pro rata* share of total sales (Y/m) and employing its *pro rata* share of labour (L/m), we will have from (V.b.3) a total demand for labour of

$$L = ml = \frac{Y}{w}\cdot\frac{\beta(1-s)}{1+\pi}. \qquad \text{V.b.5}$$

There are then two possible cases. If we express by L^* the number of workers available for employment, we will have some unemployment or some excess demand for labour according as the wage rate is set above or below the level (w^*) at which the labour market would be cleared. That is to say

$$L \lesseqgtr L^*$$

as

$$w \gtreqless w^* = (1-s)\lambda^* = (1-s)\frac{Y}{L^*}\frac{\beta}{1+\pi}. \qquad \text{V.b.6}$$

In the present section we will assume $w > w^*$ so that there is some unemployment. We will consider the case of $w < w^*$ in the following section.

A similar analysis can be carried out for the profit–sharing arrangement. With s, w, and h constant, differentiation of (V.a.4) gives

$$d\bar{q}_k = \{(1-s)x - (h'' - sh)\}\, d\bar{k} + \{(1-s)\lambda - (1-s)w\}\, d\bar{l} \qquad \text{V.b.7}$$

so that the individual firm will have an incentive to invest in more capital so long as

$$\bar{k} < \frac{1-s}{1-\phi s}\frac{\bar{x}\bar{p}}{h''}\frac{\alpha}{1+\bar{\pi}}, \qquad \text{V.b.8}$$

where $\phi = h/h''$, and to employ more labour so long as

$$l < \frac{\bar{x}\bar{p}}{w}\frac{\beta}{1+\bar{\pi}}. \quad \text{V.b.9}$$

In this case the monetary authorities must set interest rates so that

$$h'' = \frac{1-s}{1-\phi s}\frac{Y}{K^*}\frac{\alpha}{1+\pi} \quad \text{V.b.10}$$

and we will have

$$L \lesseqgtr L^*$$

as

$$w \gtreqless w^* = \lambda^* = \frac{Y}{L^*}\frac{\beta}{1+\pi}. \quad \text{V.b.11}$$

With each firm simultaneously in equilibrium, the basic structural equations for the revenue–sharing and for the profit–sharing economies take the form shown in equations (V.b.12 to 18), which can be rearranged as in equations (V.b.19 to 25) to show the ways in which the variables k, l, x, p, h'', w', and q_k are determined in terms of K^*, α, β, μ, H, Y, s, w and h (with $\pi = \mu H/m$, $\gamma = \alpha + \beta - 1$ and $\phi = h/h''$). From these one can derive $L = ml$ and $X = mx$.

In order to understand the main influences at work and the main differences between the outcomes it is useful to start by comparing some of the results with those which would occur in the case of the Capitalist Wage Economy of Chapter III. Some of the basic comparisons are made in equations (V.b.26 to 31).

Equations (V.b.26) express the relationship between the market hire–charge for a unit of capital (h'') and the marginal revenue product of that capital (x). In the wage economy investment will be expanded until the x has fallen to equality with h''. In the revenue–sharing economy, the net return to the capitalist will be only the capitalist's share of any addition to the revenue, so that the expansion of investment will cease at a point at which the charge for a unit of capital h'' is still only $(1-s)$ times the marginal revenue product x. This will also be the result in the profit–sharing economy if the

	Revenue Sharing	*Profit Sharing*	
$mxp =$	Y		V.b.12
$mk =$	K^*		13
$k =$	$(1-s)\dfrac{xp}{h''}\dfrac{\alpha}{1+\pi}$	$\dfrac{1-s}{1-\phi s}\dfrac{xp}{h''}\dfrac{\alpha}{1+\pi}$	14
$l =$	$(1-s)\dfrac{xp}{w}\dfrac{\beta}{1+\pi}$	$\dfrac{xp}{w}\cdot\dfrac{\beta}{1+\pi}$	15
$x =$	$k^{\alpha}l^{\beta}$		16
$w' =$	$w+\dfrac{sxp}{l}$	$w+\dfrac{s(xp-wl-hk)}{l}$	17
$q_k =$	$(1-s)xp-wl-h''k$	$(1-s)(xp-wl)-(1-\phi s)h''k$	18

Equations V.b.12 to 18

fixed–interest element in the return on capital (h) were zero (with $\phi = h/h'' = 0$). Once again the capitalist would receive only $(1-s)$ times the capital's marginal revenue product. But if at the other extreme the fixed–interest element in the return on capital were equal to the market hire–charge for capital ($h = h''$ and $\phi = 1$), the capitalist would receive in this form of fixed interest an amount equal to the whole of the hire–charge, which sum would be deducted from the firm's revenue before calculation of the accounting profit which had to be shared with the wage earners. In any intermediate case (with $0 < \phi < 1$) investment would be carried on up to a point at which $(1-s)x < h'' < x$.

It must be borne in mind that we are assuming that the monetary authorities will adjust the hire–charge h'' so that in all three cases the same total amount of capital K^* will be employed. Equations (V.b.26) are therefore determinants of what the hire–charge h'' will be rather

	Revenue Sharing	Profit Sharing	
$k =$	K^*/m		V.b.19
$l =$	$(1-s)\dfrac{Y}{mw}\dfrac{\beta}{1+\pi}$	$\dfrac{Y}{mw}\dfrac{\beta}{1+\pi}$	20
$x =$	$\left(\dfrac{K^*}{m}\right)^{\alpha}\left([1-s]\dfrac{Y}{mw}\dfrac{\beta}{1+\pi}\right)^{\beta}$	$\left(\dfrac{K}{m}\right)^{\alpha}\left(\dfrac{Y}{mw}\dfrac{\beta}{1+\pi}\right)^{\beta}$	21
$p =$	$\dfrac{Y}{m}\left(\dfrac{K^*}{m}\right)^{-\alpha}\left([1-s]\dfrac{Y}{mw}\dfrac{\beta}{1+\pi}\right)^{-\beta}$	$\dfrac{Y}{m}\left(\dfrac{K}{m}\right)^{-\alpha}\left(\dfrac{Y}{mw}\dfrac{\beta}{1+\pi}\right)^{-\beta}$	22
$h'' =$	$(1-s)\dfrac{Y}{K''}\dfrac{\alpha}{1+\pi}$	$\dfrac{1-s}{1-\phi s}\dfrac{Y}{K^*}\dfrac{\alpha}{1+\pi}$	23
$w' =$	$w\left\{1+\dfrac{s}{\beta}\dfrac{1+\pi}{1-s}\right\}$	$w\left\{1+\dfrac{s}{\beta}\left(1+\pi-\beta-\alpha\phi\dfrac{1-s}{1-\phi s}\right)\right\}$	24
	$(1-s)\dfrac{Y}{m}\dfrac{\pi-\gamma}{1+\pi}$		25

Note: Y, K^*, α, β, γ, m, and π can be assumed to have the same values in both columns, but there is no reason to assume that the pay parameters s and w will be the same for both columns.

Equations V.b.19 to 25

than of the level of the marginal revenue product of capital (x). Indeed in our model the combination of the production function assumed in Section (c) of Chapter II, of the market structure assumed in Section (a) of Chapter II, and of the demand–management structure assumed in Section (d) of Chapter II means that the absolute value of $x = (Y/K^*)(\alpha/[1+\pi])$ will be the same in all three columns of (V.b.26). The production function implies that the marginal product of capital will be α times its average product x/k. The market structure implies that, given the number of firms m, the marginal revenue

	Wage Economy	*Revenue Sharing*	*Profit Sharing*	
$h'' =$	x	$(1-s)x$	$\frac{1-s}{1-\phi s}x$	V.b.26
$w =$	λ	$(1-s)\lambda$	λ	27
$w' - w =$	0	$w\frac{s}{\beta}\frac{1+\pi}{1-s}$	$w\frac{s}{\beta}\left(1+\pi-\beta-\alpha\phi\frac{1-s}{1-\phi s}\right)$	28
$\frac{w}{\lambda}$	1	$1-s$	1	29
$\frac{w'}{\lambda}$	1	$1+\frac{s}{\beta}(1+\pi-\beta)$	$1+\frac{s}{\beta}\left(1+\pi-\beta-\alpha\phi\frac{1-s}{1-\phi s}\right)$	30
q_k	$\frac{Y}{m}\frac{\pi-\gamma}{1+\pi}$	$(1-s)\frac{Y}{m}\frac{\pi-\gamma}{1+\pi}$	$(1-s)\frac{Y}{m}\frac{\pi-\gamma}{1+\pi}$	31

Note: $Y, m, \alpha, \beta, \gamma, \pi$ and $x = (Y/K^*)(\alpha/([1+\pi])$ have the same values in all three columns. $\lambda = (Y/L)(\beta/[1+\pi])$, s, w, and w' are not assumed to have the same values in all the columns.

Equations V.b.26 to 31

will be $1/(1+\pi)$ times the price of the product p. The demand management structure implies that each firm will receive a revenue equal to $xp = Y/m$. As a result we have $x = (\alpha)(x/k)(p/[1+\pi]) = (Y/K^*)(\alpha/[1+\pi])$. It is not assumed that x and p will be the same in all three columns. The composition of Y between output and prices may differ; but with the assumptions of our model this composition will not affect the value of x.

This result is not the same for the marginal revenue product of labour which is considered in equations (V.b.27). Since $\lambda = (Y/L)(\beta/[1+\pi])$ the value of λ will depend upon L as well as the constants Y, β and π; and in the absence of any assumption that there must be full employment ($L = L^*$) it is not assumed that the choice of institutional arrangements will have no effect on employment. Indeed when we come on to discuss equations (V.b.29 and 30), it will be shown that L and so λ may differ in important respects as between the three different institutional arrangements.

In all three cases the full–employment value of the marginal revenue product would be the same, namely $\lambda^* = (Y/L^*)(\beta/[1+\pi])$. But the full–employment wage rate, w^*, will not be the same in all three cases. For full employment we would in fact have $w \leqslant w^* = \lambda^*$ in the wage economy and in the profit–sharing economy but $w \leqslant w^* = (1-s)\lambda^*$ in the revenue–sharing economy (see V.b.6). In the wage economy labour will be employed up to the point at which the fixed–wage rate is equal to labour's marginal revenue product ($w = \lambda$). This will also be the case in the profit–sharing economy. In this case the fixed–wage rate is deducted from the accounting profit, so that it is only the excess of labour's marginal revenue product over the fixed–wage rate that the capitalist has to share with the worker. Since the capitalist will get his share $(1-s)$ of this excess he will expand employment so long as the excess is positive, even though he is not, as in the wage economy, receiving the whole of that excess. In the revenue–sharing economy the capitalist receives only his share $(1-s)$ of the whole of labour's marginal revenue product and will, therefore, have an incentive to employ labour only up to the point at which $w = (1-s)\lambda$.

In equations (V.b.28) we measure the share element $(w' - w)$ in the worker's inclusive rate of pay (w') as a multiple of the fixed–wage element (w). This is, of course, zero in the wage economy in which there is no share element. It is necessarily positive in the revenue–sharing economy in which one assumes that a firm will not exist unless it produces some positive net value–added. In the profit–sharing economy it will be positive only so long as the firm's accounting profit is positive.

There is, of course, no suggestion that either the share ratio, s, or the fixed wage, w, will necessarily be the same in the profit–sharing economy as in the revenue–sharing economy. But simply as a means of understanding the influences at work it is instructive to consider three reasons why, if s and w were the same in the two cases, the share element $(w' - w)$ would be higher in the revenue–sharing than in the profit–sharing economy.

From (V.b.17) we have

$$\left.\begin{array}{ll} w' - w = \dfrac{sxp}{l} \text{ with revenue–sharing} & \\ \text{and} & \\ w' - w = \dfrac{sxp}{l} - sw - s\dfrac{hk}{l} \text{ with profit–sharing} & \end{array}\right\} \quad \text{V.b.32}$$

for the revenue–sharing and the profit–sharing economies respectively.

From (V.b.15) it can be seen that, at any given value of w, revenue per worker (xp/l) will be higher in the revenue–sharing economy $(w[1+\pi]/\beta[1-s])$ than in the profit–sharing economy $(w[1+\pi]/\beta)$, because in the former case the sacrifice of a proportion s of labour's marginal revenue product will reduce the employment of labour and will maintain average output at a higher level. This is the first reason why, with any given level of w, $(w' - w)$ will be higher in the former than in the latter case.

The other two reasons are that the accounting profit which is to be shared in the profit–sharing economy will be lower than the total revenue to be shared in the revenue–sharing economy, because of the deduction of wl and hk from the accounting profit. For each individual worker this means a reduction in the share element in his pay of sw and of $sh(k/l)$, which latter element can from (V.b.14 and 15), be seen to be equal to $(sw/\beta)(\alpha\phi[1-s]/[1-\phi s])$.

These three factors account for (1) the absence of the term $(1-s)$, (2) the presence of the term $(-\beta)$, and (3) the presence of the term $(-(\alpha\phi)([1-s]/[1-\phi s]))$ in the value of $(w' - w)$ for the profit–sharing economy as compared with that for the revenue–sharing economy, as given in (V.b.28). It is to be noted that if $h = h''$ (i.e. if $\phi = 1$) the share element in the profit–sharing economy would be $w(s/\beta)(\pi - \gamma)$, which means that the share element would be reduced to zero unless $\pi > \gamma$ i.e. unless there were an element of structural profit due to the fact that market conditions allowed the mark–up of selling price on marginal revenue (π) to exceed the mark–up of average cost on marginal cost (γ) necessitated by the production function.

The choice of institutional arrangement as between wage economy, revenue–sharing and profit–sharing can have a significant effect upon the level of employment. The easiest way to consider these employment effects is to stand the question on its head and to ask what differences there must be in rates of pay in order to obtain the same level of employment in the different institutional arrangements. If case A requires a lower rate of pay in order to achieve the same level of employment as in case B, we may infer that at the same rate of pay the level of employment would be lower in case A than in case B.

Equations (V.b.29 and 30) which are directly derived from equations (V.b.27 and 28) can serve for this analysis. In all cases we will have from (II.c.15) $\lambda = (Y/L)(\beta/[1 + \pi])$ so that for L to be the same in all three cases, we can assume that λ will be the same in all three cases. It follows from (V.b.29) that for employment to be the same as in the wage economy case, the fixed–wage rate element in pay in the revenue–sharing case must be only $(1 - s)$ times its level in the wage economy case, whereas in the profit–sharing case it can be as high as in the wage economy case. Alternatively we can interpret this as saying that if the fixed–wage element of pay were the same in all three cases, the level of employment would be the same in the profit–sharing case as in the wage economy case, but would be lower than this in the revenue–sharing case.

On the other hand, from equations (V.b.30) we can deduce that with employment the same in all three cases there will be a higher inclusive rate of pay in the revenue–sharing case than in the wage economy case, or, alternatively, that with the same inclusive rate of pay employment would be higher in the revenue–sharing case than in the wage economy case. The same conclusion would be reached for the comparison of the profit–sharing case with the wage economy case except in the special conditions where $\phi = 1$ and $\pi = \gamma$ in which case the outcome would be the same in the profit–sharing case as in the wage economy case.

It is interesting to see why in the revenue–sharing case a lower fixed rate of wage (w) but a higher inclusive rate of pay (w') than in the wage economy case is needed to maintain the same level of employment.

If one takes on one more unit of labour in the revenue–sharing firm one adds $w + s\lambda$ to the labour cost, because a proportion s of the marginal revenue product λ as well as the fixed wage w will accrue to labour. At the same time one adds λ to the total revenue, so that one employs labour up to the point at which

$$\left.\begin{array}{l} w + s\lambda = \lambda \\ \text{with} \\ w = (1 - s)\lambda < \lambda \end{array}\right\} \qquad \text{V.b.33}$$

The inclusive rate of pay is, however, $w + (sxp/l)$. With $\lambda = (xp/l)(\beta/[1 + \pi])$ we have $\lambda < xp/l$ (i.e. the marginal revenue product is < average revenue product) so that

$$w' = w + \frac{sxp}{l} > w + s\lambda = \lambda. \qquad \text{V.b.34}$$

Thus we have

$$\frac{Y}{L} > w' > \lambda > w > 0. \qquad \text{V.b.35}$$

The first and the last terms in (V.b.35) are added, because the inclusive rate of pay cannot be set so as to absorb the whole or more than the whole of the firm's revenue, while the fixed wage rate must be greater than zero. Thus the inclusive rate of pay will lie between the average and the marginal revenue product and the fixed wage will lie between the marginal revenue product and zero.

From (V.b.31) it can be seen that the capitalist profit, q_K, both in the revenue–sharing and in the profit–sharing case will be equal to $(1 - s)(Y/m)([\pi - \gamma]/[1 + \pi])$, i.e. to $(1 - s)$ times any element of structural profit due to the excess of the price mark–up allowed by the market conditions (π) over the average cost mark–up (γ) on marginal cost. In the wage economy the capitalist profit would be equal to the structural profit. This means that in conditions in which the structural profit would be zero (i.e. in which $\pi = \gamma$) capitalist profit would be zero in all three cases of wage economy, revenue–sharing economy, and profit–sharing economy. The factors at work in leading to this result can be understood in the following way.

A basic feature of the sharing arrangements is a potential shift of the distribution of the revenue of the firm as between worker's income and capitalist's income, equations (V.b.26) showing how the reward of capital (h'') may be reduced below its marginal revenue product and equations (V.b.27 and 28) showing how the inclusive pay of labour may be raised above its marginal revenue product. The rise in the inclusive pay of workers represents a rise in costs; but the reduction in the hire–charge for capital, while it represents a reduction in the incomes of the general body of capitalists, represents also a reduction in costs of production. In fact if $\pi = \gamma$ the rise in labour costs is exactly balanced by the fall in capital costs.

We can express the rise in labour costs above what they would have been if labour had been paid its marginal revenue product as $(w' - \lambda)l$. In the revenue–sharing case, using (V.b.17 and 27) and (II.c.15), we obtain:

$$\begin{aligned}(w' - \lambda)l &= (w' - w)l - (\lambda - w)l \\ &= sxp - s\lambda l \\ &= sxp\left(1 - \frac{\beta}{1+\pi}\right). \qquad \text{V.b.36}\end{aligned}$$

Similarly we can express the fall in capital costs below what they would be if capital were paid its marginal revenue product as $(h'' - \varkappa)k$. In the revenue–sharing case, using (V.b.26) and (II.c.15), we have

$$\begin{aligned}(h'' - \varkappa)k &= -s\varkappa k \\ &= -sxp\frac{\alpha}{1+\pi}. \qquad \text{V.b.37}\end{aligned}$$

Thus we have

$$(w' - \lambda)l + (h'' - \varkappa)k = sxp\frac{\pi - \gamma}{1+\pi}, \qquad \text{V.b.38}$$

which shows that there will be a net rise in costs equal to a fraction, s, of structural profit, if any such profit exists. As a result the capitalist's profit will be reduced from the structural profit in the wage economy case to $(1-s)$ times that profit in the revenue–sharing case.

A similar analysis is relevant in the profit–sharing case. In this case, using (V.b.17, 27, 14, and 15) we obtain

$$\begin{aligned}(w'-\lambda)l &= (w'-w)l-(\lambda-w)l\\ &= s(xp-wl-hk)-0\\ &= sxp\left(1-\frac{\beta}{1+\pi}-\frac{1-s}{1-\phi s}\cdot\frac{\alpha\phi}{1+\pi}\right).\end{aligned} \qquad \text{V.b.39}$$

Similarly using (V.b.14) and (II.c.15) we obtain

$$\begin{aligned}(h''-x)k &= h''k-xk\\ &= \frac{1-s}{1-\phi s}xp\frac{\alpha}{1+\pi}-xp\frac{\alpha}{1+\pi}\\ &= -sxp\frac{\alpha}{1+\pi}\frac{1-\phi}{1-\phi s}.\end{aligned} \qquad \text{V.b.40}$$

It follows that once again

$$(w'-\lambda)h+(h''-x)k = sxp\frac{\pi-\gamma}{1+\pi}. \qquad \text{V.b.41}$$

Thus in the profit–sharing as well as in the revenue–sharing case we reach the conclusions (1) that in the absence of any structural profit the capitalists' profit will remain at zero as in the wage economy but (2) that in the presence of a structural profit the capitalists will lose a proportion of s of that profit which they would have enjoyed in its entirety in the wage economy.

(c) The Capitalist Sharing Economy with Rigid Pay Parameters and Full Employment

We turn now to the analysis of a situation which is similar to the one examined in Section (b) in that the pay parameters are assumed to be rigidly fixed at w and s, but which is dissimilar in that w is assumed to be set at so low a level ($w \leqslant w^*$) that there is now full employment ($L = L^*$) in the economy. As can be seen from (V.b.6 and 11) this means that

$$w \leqslant w^* = (1-s)\lambda^* = (1-s)\frac{Y}{L^*}\frac{\beta}{1+\pi} \qquad \text{V.c.1}$$

in the revenue–sharing economy and that

$$w \leqslant w^* = \lambda^* = \frac{Y}{L^*}\cdot\frac{\beta}{1+\pi} \qquad \text{V.c.2}$$

in the profit–sharing economy.

In the analysis of full employment in the wage economy in Section (d) of Chapter III we considered only the case in which $w = w^*$ and neglected the possibility that $w < w^*$ on the grounds that one could assume that forces of competition between employers or of trade union bargaining would drive the wage rate up at least to the full–employment level. But in examining the institutions of revenue–sharing and of profit–sharing one cannot neglect the possibility that $w < w^*$. Indeed, in the case of pure revenue–sharing arrangements we have $w = 0$ with the whole of the inclusive pay of the worker taking the form of a share element (sY/L).

With $w < w^*$ there will be an excess demand for labour in each firm. In the rest of this section we will assume that each firm, being for some unspecified reason bound to offer the same rigidly fixed payment terms of w and s, manages to attract the same amount of labour even though at these fixed pay parameters each firm would like to take on more labour, so that

$$l = \frac{L^*}{m}. \qquad \text{V.c.3}$$

This is an arbitrary and uncomfortable assumption and represents a fortuitous and unstable situation, and in this respect the situation discussed in this section differs in an important respect from the situation discussed in the previous section, in which every firm was content with the amount of labour which it was employing at the given rigidly fixed pay parameters.

One of the main, if not the main, claim made for the merits of a share economy rests upon the assumption that in one sense or another there exists an excess demand for labour. It is this feature of the situation which justifies the claim that if there is a fall in demand the impact effect in a share economy will be a reduction in money prices, profits, and wage incomes rather than in employment and output, as would be the case in a wage economy with a rigidly fixed wage rate. But this advantage will exist in a share economy with rigidly fixed pay parameters only if the fixed–wage element in pay (w) is set below its full–employment level (w^*). If this were not the case a fall in demand for the firm's product would lead to a reduction in employment and output just as in the wage economy. The assumption that w may be less than w^* is thus an essential feature for the analysis of the share economy with rigid pay parameters.

A possible resolution of these problems arising from the assumption that w may be less than w^* will be discussed below in Section (f) where we consider the possibility of flexibility in the parameters w and s. For the rest of this section we simply accept the existence of rigidly fixed pay parameters and the consequences which result if w is set below w^*.

The structural equations for the economy will now be as given in equations (V.c.4 to 11) which can be rearranged as in (V.c.12 to 19) to show how each of the variables k, l, x, p, h'', w^*, w' and q_k is determined in terms of the parameters K^*, m, L^*, α, β, s, Y, ϕ, w, μ, and H with $\pi = \mu H/m$ and $\gamma = \alpha + \beta - 1$. By comparison of (V.c.12, 13, 14, and 15) with (III.d.10, 11, 12 and 13) it can be seen that the 'real' variables k, l, and x and the general price level p are the same in full–employment conditions in the share economy as in the wage economy. It is the distribution variables h'', w^*, w', and q_k which in full employment are affected by the choice of institutional arrangement. These effects are best considered by the rearrangement of the terms as given in (V.c.20 to 25).

If $w = w^*$, i.e. if $\theta = 1$, then the results given in (V.c.20 to 25) are the same as the corresponding results given in (V.b.26 to 31) for the situation in conditions of unemployment with the sole difference that, λ is set at λ^* for all three columns, and w is set at $w^* = \lambda^*$ for the wage

	Revenue Sharing	Profit Sharing	
$mxp =$	Y		V.c.4
$mk =$	K^*		5
$k =$	$(1-s)\dfrac{xp}{h''}\cdot\dfrac{\alpha}{1+\pi}$	$\dfrac{1-s}{1-\phi s}\cdot\dfrac{xp}{h''}\dfrac{\alpha}{1+\pi}$	6
$ml =$	L^*		7
$x =$	$k^\alpha l^\beta$		8
$w^* =$	$(1-s)\dfrac{Y}{L^*}\dfrac{\beta}{1+\pi}$	$\dfrac{Y}{L^*}\dfrac{\beta}{1+\pi}$	9
$w' - w =$	$\dfrac{sxp}{l}$	$\dfrac{s(xp-wl-hk)}{l}$	10
$q_k =$	$(1-s)xp - wl - h''k$	$(1-s)(xp-wl)-(1-\phi s)h''k$	11

Equations V.c.4 to 11

economy and the profit–sharing economy, and at $w^* = (1-s)\lambda$ for the revenue–sharing economy. We would in effect be in a situation similar to that analysed in Section (b) in which w was set at a level in each column which happened to lead to a demand for labour equal to the particular value of L^*. There is really no more to be added in useful commentary.

The situation is different when w is set below w^* and the effect appears in equations (V.c.20 to 25) by the presence of the term θ. The values of w/λ, w'/λ and q_k are the ones which are significantly affected and a comparison of their full–employment values in

	Revenue Sharing	Profit Sharing	
$k =$	$\frac{K^*}{m}$		V.c.12
$l =$	$\frac{L^*}{m}$		13
$x =$	$\left(\frac{K^*}{m}\right)^{\alpha}\left(\frac{L^*}{m}\right)^{\beta}$		14
$p =$	$\frac{Y}{m}\cdot\left(\frac{K^*}{m}\right)^{-\alpha}\left(\frac{L^*}{m}\right)^{-\beta}$		15
$h'' =$	$(1-s)\frac{Y}{K^*}\cdot\frac{\alpha}{1+\pi}$	$\frac{1-s}{1-\phi s}\cdot\frac{Y}{K^*}\frac{\alpha}{1+\pi}$	16
$w^* =$	$(1-s)\frac{Y}{L^*}\cdot\frac{\beta}{1+\pi}$	$\frac{Y}{L^*}\frac{\beta}{1+\pi}$	17
$w' =$	$w+\frac{sY}{L^*}$	$w(1-s)+\frac{sY}{L^*}\left\{1-\frac{1-s}{1-\phi s}\frac{\alpha\phi}{1+\pi}\right\}$	18
$q_k =$	$(1-s)\frac{Y}{m}\cdot\frac{\pi-\gamma+\beta}{1+\pi}-\frac{wL^*}{m}$	$(1-s)\frac{Y}{m}\cdot\frac{\pi-\gamma+\beta}{1+\pi}-(1-s)\frac{wL^*}{m}$	19

(The expressions for k, l, x and p are common to both revenue sharing and profit sharing.)

Equations V.c.12 to 19

(V.c.23, 24 and 25) with their unemployment values in (V.b.29, 30 and 31) brings out the essential features of the new situation.

The ratio w/λ is assumed to remain set at unity in the wage economy because it is assumed that w does not fall below w^*. But in both the revenue–sharing and the profit–sharing economy the ratio w/λ in the

	Wage Economy	*Revenue Sharing*	*Profit Sharing*	
$h'' =$	x	$(1-s)x$	$\frac{1-s}{1-\phi s}x$	V.c.20
$w^* =$	λ^*	$(1-s)\lambda^*$	λ^*	21
$w' - w =$	0	$w^* \frac{s}{\beta} \cdot \frac{1+\pi}{1+s}$	$w^* \frac{s}{\beta}\left(1+\pi-\theta\beta-\alpha\phi\frac{1-s}{1-\phi s}\right)$	22
$\frac{w}{\lambda^*} =$	1	$(1-s)\theta$	θ	23
$\frac{w'}{\lambda^*} =$	1	$(1-s)\theta + \frac{s}{\beta}(1+\pi)$	$\theta(1-s) + \frac{s}{\beta}\left(1+\pi-\alpha\phi\frac{1-s}{1-\phi s}\right)$	24
$q_k =$	$\frac{Y}{m} \cdot \frac{\pi-\gamma}{1+\pi}$	$(1-s)\frac{Y}{m} \cdot \frac{\pi-\gamma+\beta(1-\theta)}{1+\pi}$	$(1-s)\frac{Y}{m} \cdot \frac{\pi-\gamma+\beta(1-\theta)}{1+\pi}$	25

where $\lambda^* = \frac{Y}{L^*}\frac{\beta}{1+\pi}$ and $\theta = \frac{w}{w^*}$

Equations V.c.20 to 25

full–employment situation is only a fraction θ of its value in the unemployment situation.

The ratio w'/λ is similarly assumed to stay set at unity in the wage economy. But in both the revenue–sharing and the profit–sharing economies this ratio is reduced by an absolute amount equal to $(1-\theta)(1-s)$ when one moves from unemployment to full–employment conditions. We saw (in V.b.35) that in the unemployment situation in the revenue–sharing economy we would necessarily have $w' > \lambda$. This is no longer the case. If θ and s are both sufficiently low we can have $w' < \lambda$ in (V.c.24). Consider the pure revenue–sharing case in which $\theta = 0$. Then from (V.c.24) we would have $w' < \lambda$, if $s < \beta/(1+\pi)$. The meaning of this is clear. $\beta/(1+\pi)$ represents the proportion of the firm's revenue which would accrue to labour if labour were paid its marginal revenue product ($\lambda^* = (xp/l)(\beta/[1+\pi])$), while s represents the proportion of the firm's revenue which will accrue to labour if labour received pay only in the form of a share of revenue ($w' = sxp/l$). In the absence of a fixed–wage element w, we would thus have $w'/\lambda < 1$ if $s < \beta/(1+\pi)$.

If $\theta < 1$, there can be very important effects upon the level of the capitalists' profit as shown in (V.b.19 and 25). It is clear from (V.b.25) that if $\theta = 1$, then the capitalists' profit remains in both the revenue–sharing and the profit–sharing case the same in full–employment as in unemployment conditions, namely a fraction $(1-s)$ of any structural profit $((Y/m)([\pi-\gamma]/[1+\pi]))$. But as θ falls below unity, the reduction of w below the level needed to ensure full employment adds an extra bonus of profit.

The way in which this affects q_k can be seen very clearly if one assumes a pure share economy with w set at zero and the pay of labour taking the form only of a share element.

In the revenue–sharing case the reduction of w from w^* to zero causes a reduction of w^*l in the cost of labour. But in this case we have $w^* = (1-s)l^*$ so that the reduction in cost is $(1-s)\lambda^*l$. But $\lambda^*l = xp(\beta/[1+\pi]) = (Y/m)(\beta/[1+\pi])$. Thus the capitalists gain $(1-s)(Y/m)(\beta/[1+\pi])$.

In the profit-sharing case when the wage rate w falls from w^* to zero the capitalists gain only $(1-s)w^*l$ because q_a is increased by w^*l so that the workers obtain their share (s) of this increase in the accounting profit (w^*l). But in this case we have $w^* = \lambda^*$ so that once more the gain to the capitalists is $(1-s)\lambda^*l = (1-s)(Y/m)(\beta/[1+\pi])$.

If one adds this gain to the profit which the capitalists would have received when $w = w^*$ we obtain

$$q_k = (1-s)\frac{Y}{m}\frac{\pi-\gamma}{1+\pi} + (1-s)\frac{Y}{m}\frac{\beta}{1+\pi} = (1-s)\frac{Y}{m}\frac{\pi-\gamma+\beta}{1+\pi}.$$

The actual gain will be only a fraction $(1-\theta)$ times the gain from setting w at zero if in fact the wage rate is set at θw^*, which explains the formulation of q_k in (V.c.25).

This effect upon q_k can have very far-reaching implications as will become clear in the following section.

(d) The Effect of Rigid Pay Parameters on the Number of Firms

If $w > w^*$ so that $L < L^*$ in both the revenue–sharing economy and the profit–sharing economy, the capitalists' profit will be equal to $(1-s)$ times the firm's structural profit $(Y/m)([\pi-\gamma]/[1+\pi])$ as is shown in (V.b.25). If new firms enter the market so long as the capitalists' profit is positive, we will have m increasing so long as $\pi > \gamma$ so that the equilibrium number of firms will settle at

$$\tilde{m} = \frac{\mu H}{\gamma}, \qquad \text{V.d.1}$$

which has the same value as that given for the Capitalist Wage Economy in (III.c.3).

Moreover in the unemployment conditions with $w > w^*$ the number of firms which would be attracted into the economy in both the revenue–sharing and the profit–sharing economies would be the same as the number attracted into the Capitalist Wage Economy even if the entry of new firms were determined on the principles discussed in the note at the end of Section (c) of Chapter III.

From (V.b.18) we can express the capitalists' profit as

$$q_k = (1-s)xp - wl - h''k \qquad \text{V.d.2}$$

in the revenue–sharing case and as

$$q_k = (1-s)xp - (1-s)wl - (1-\phi s)h''k \qquad \text{V.d.3}$$

in the profit–sharing case. Thus in terms of equation (III.c.25) we have

$$\zeta_1 = (1-s),\ \zeta_2 = 1,\ \text{and}\ \zeta_3 = 1 \qquad \text{V.d.4}$$

in the revenue–sharing case and

$$\zeta_1 = (1-s),\ \zeta_2 = (1-s),\ \text{and}\ \zeta_3 = (1-\phi s) \qquad \text{V.d.5}$$

in the profit–sharing case. But as shown in the note at the end of Chapter III, the values of these ζ parameters make no difference to the result that the equilibrium number of firms will be given by the solution of equation (III.c.35), namely:

$$(1+\pi)\left(\frac{1+\pi}{\pi}\right)^{\gamma} e^{\pi/2} = (1+\gamma)\left(\frac{1+\gamma}{\gamma}\right)^{\gamma} e^{\gamma} \qquad \text{V.d.6}$$

where

$$m = \frac{\mu H}{\pi}.$$

If $w < w^*$ so that with rigid pay parameters, s and w, there is an excess demand for labour in the revenue–sharing and the profit–sharing economies, there may be an upper limit to the number of firms which can exist in the market and yet make a non–zero capitalists' profit. But below any such upper limit the actual number of firms is in effect arbitrary. We have arbitrarily assumed that when there is an excess demand for labour each firm will happen to employ the same number of workers L/m; but it remains an equally arbitrary matter whether or not one assumes that in these conditions any additional firm could or could not automatically attract, at the same rigidly given pay parameters (s and w), its 'quota' of labour, namely $L/(m+1)$.

However, there remains the question whether there is any upper limit set by profitability to the number of firms which can continue to operate in the full–employment revenue–sharing or profit–sharing economies. From (V.c.25) we see that the number of firms could increase and still operate at a profit so long as

$$\pi > \gamma - \beta(1-\theta) = \beta\theta - (1-\alpha). \qquad \text{V.d.7}$$

If $\theta > (1-\alpha)/\beta$,[1] this means that an upper limit to the number of firms will be set by $\pi = \gamma - \beta(1-\theta)$, i.e. at

$$\tilde{m} = \frac{\mu H}{\gamma - \beta(1-\theta)}. \qquad \text{V.d.8}$$

If one compares this with the value for $\tilde{m}$ in (III.c.3), it is clear that this upper-limit number of firms in the capitalist revenue–sharing economy with full employment will exceed the equilibrium number of firms in the capitalist fixed–wage economy where $\tilde{m} = \mu H/\gamma$, a value which already exceeds the optimal value as given for $\hat{m}$ in (III.d.27).

But θ can lie at any value between 0 and 1 and we might well have $\theta < (1-\alpha)/\beta$. This would certainly be the case in a pure revenue–sharing economy with a zero value for the fixed wage w and so for θ. But since $\pi = \mu H/m$ is always > 0 but approaches zero as m approaches infinity, we can see from (V.d.7) that, with $\theta < (1-\alpha)/\beta$, there would be no upper limit to the number of firms.

This result would be avoided if we had used a production function of the kind mentioned in the footnote on page 19, since a fixed overhead cost would prevent the size of the firm from falling below some lower limit. But the implications for an excessive number of firms in equilibrium conditions would remain.

We are left then with two disturbing features of a capitalist sharing economy with fixed pay parameters which lead to full employment and an excess demand for labour.

First, the distribution of the factors between the individual firms would be arbitrary and perhaps unstable since every firm would be seeking to employ more than its *pro rata* share of the total supply of labour.

Second the number of firms would be arbitrary, subject only to a possible upper limit which would in any case greatly exceed the optimal number.

In the following sections of this chapter we will modify the assumption of the rigidity of the pay parameters s and w and show how different degrees of flexibility in these parameters would remove these disturbing features.

[1] Since $\alpha + \beta > 1$, $1 - \alpha < \beta$. Thus with $\alpha < 1$ we have $0 < (1-\alpha)/\beta < 1$. $\theta = w/w^*$ must lie between 0 and 1 in order to ensure an excess demand for labour, if we rule out the possibility of a negative fixed wage rate.

(e) Competition with Fixed–Wage Firms

In this section we will maintain the assumption that for all revenue–sharing firms the pay parameters s and w are rigidly fixed. But we will assume that if a fixed–wage firm were set up and were willing and able to pay an inclusive rate of pay ($w'_w = w_w$) which was at least as high as the inclusive rate of pay offered in the revenue–sharing firms ($w'_s = w_s + sxp/l$), there would be no obstacle to its doing so.

Consider then a revenue–sharing firm which converts itself into a fixed–wage firm. As in (V.a.2) its profit can be expressed as

$$\bar{q}_k = \bar{x}\bar{p} - w'\bar{l} - h''\bar{k}. \qquad \text{V.e.1}$$

With w' and h'' constant, differentiation gives

$$d\bar{q}_k = (x - h'')\, d\bar{k} + (\lambda - w')\, d\bar{l}, \qquad \text{V.e.2}$$

where λ and x have the values given in (II.c.15). The firm can now clearly increase its profit by investing in more capital equipment since in the surrounding revenue–sharing regime

$$h'' = (1 - s)x < x. \qquad \text{V.e.3}$$

In its fixed–wage form it does not need to pay any share of capital's marginal revenue product to labour; and it will therefore pay it to take advantage of the very cheap hire–charge for capital by increasing its investment.

If the surrounding revenue–sharing regime is one with unemployment, we would have from (V.b.30)

$$w' = \lambda\left\{1 + \frac{s}{\beta}(1 + \pi - \beta)\right\} > \lambda. \qquad \text{V.e.4}$$

In this case the fixed–wage firm could increase its profit at the same inclusive rate of pay still further by taking on less labour. It would then in fact have reduced its costs by substituting capital (for which the hire–charge was below its marginal revenue product) for labour (for which the inclusive rate of pay was above its marginal revenue product).

If the surrounding revenue–sharing regime was one with full

employment, we would have from (V.c.24)

$$\frac{w'}{\lambda} = (1 - s)\theta + \frac{s}{\beta}(1 + \pi), \qquad \text{V.e.5}$$

which implies

$$w' \lesseqgtr \lambda \text{ as } \frac{s}{1 - \theta(1 - s)} \lesseqgtr \frac{\beta}{1 + \pi}, \qquad \text{V.e.6}$$

where $\beta/(1 + \pi)$ measures the proportion of the firm's revenue which would just suffice to pay labour its marginal revenue product. From (V.e.6) we can see that with $\theta = 0$ we would have $w' \lesseqgtr \lambda$ according as $s \lesseqgtr \beta/(1 + \pi)$. With $\theta = 1$, it is clear that $w' > \lambda$ since $\beta/(1 + \pi) < 1$. Thus we may have $w' \lesseqgtr \lambda$ dependent upon the relationship between θ, s, and $\beta/(1 + \pi)$ as set out in (V.e.6). Firms when they shift to the wage regime will be able to increase or decrease their profit by taking on less or more labour according as $s/(1 - \theta[1 - s]) \gtrless \beta/(1 + \pi)$.

Thus firms by shifting from a revenue–sharing to a wage regime could increase their profit by investing in more capital. In unemployment conditions they could further increase their profit by taking on less labour; and in full–employment conditions it might also be profitable for them to change the level of their employment, if necessary attracting more labour by sharing some of their extra profit with their workers and offering them, in the form of a fixed wage, a higher inclusive rate of pay than previously. But even if changes in their labour force were ruled out, they could still gain from the change by increasing their capital development.

If this profitable shift from a revenue–sharing to a fixed–wage structure was adopted by more and more firms, the demand for capital funds would rise. As a result the hire–charge for capital would have to rise above $h'' = (1 - s)x$ until, when all firms had shifted their structures, the hire–charge would rise to $h'' = x = (Y/K^*)(\alpha/[1 + \pi])$ as in (III.b.13).

At the same time the demand for labour at the current w' would fall if $w' > \lambda$ as would certainly be the case if there were already some unemployment in the economy, and might fall or rise according as $w' \gtrless \lambda$ if there were full employment in the revenue–sharing economy.

A similar though slightly more complex analysis is relevant in considering competition of wage firms with profit–sharing firms. We start once more with equations (V.e.1 and 2) but (V.e.3) is now replaced by

$$h'' = \frac{1-s}{1-\phi s} x \leqslant x \qquad \text{V.e.7}$$

and it will be profitable for the firm which shifts to a wage basis to increase investment if $\phi < 1$.

If the surrounding regime is one with unemployment, (V.e.4) is replaced by

$$w' = \lambda\left\{1 + \frac{s}{\beta}\left(1 + \pi - \beta - \alpha\phi\frac{1-s}{1-\phi s}\right)\right\}, \qquad \text{V.e.8}$$

which means that $w' > \lambda$ and it will be profitable once more to reduce employment if $\phi < 1$ or, in any case, if $\pi > \gamma$.

In a surrounding regime of full employment we would have

$$w' = \lambda\left\{(1-s)\theta + \frac{s}{\beta}\left(1 + \pi - \alpha\phi\frac{1-s}{1-\phi s}\right)\right\}, \qquad \text{V.e.9}$$

which implies

$$w' \lesseqgtr \lambda \text{ as } \frac{s}{1-\theta(1-s)} \lesseqgtr \frac{\beta}{1+\pi-\alpha\phi(1-s)/(1-\phi s)}. \qquad \text{V.e.10}$$

If $\phi = 0$ (i.e. if $h = 0$) then the condition in (V.e.10) for the profit–sharing economy is exactly the same as that in (V.e.6) for the revenue–sharing economy. At the other extreme, if $\phi = 1$ (i.e. if $h = h''$) then the condition (V.e.10) becomes

$$w' \lesseqgtr \lambda \text{ as } \frac{s}{1-\theta(1-s)} \lesseqgtr \frac{\beta}{1+\pi-\alpha} = \frac{\beta}{\beta-\pi-\gamma}, \qquad \text{V.e.11}$$

which sets a lower limit (but one which remains below unity) for the setting of $s/(1-\theta\,[1-s])$ if w' is to exceed λ. But once again w' may exceed or fall below λ, so that it may be profitable for firms which shift onto a wage basis from a profit–sharing basis to decrease or to increase their work force.

In general we may conclude that if firms on a sharing basis had to operate on rigid parameters s and w and if it were open for them to shift on to a wage basis provided that they did not reduce the inclusive rate of pay w', it would pay them to do so. The resulting increased demand for capital would necessitate a rise in the hire–charge for capital (h'') up to the value of its marginal revenue product (x) and the market for labour would be cleared either by a change in the level of employment at the given inclusive rate of pay or, in conditions in which that would imply an excess demand for labour, by a rise in the fixed wage offered (w) above the pre–existing inclusive rate of pay (w').

(f) Survival through Flexibility of the Pay Parameters

In the previous section we assumed that the pay parameters s and w were rigidly fixed (e.g. by a national wage bargain) for all capitalist enterprises which chose to organize themselves on a revenue–sharing basis; but we assumed at the same time that those capitalist enterprises which chose to organize themselves on a fixed–wage basis were free to do so provided that they paid a fixed wage (w) which was at least as high as the inclusive pay (w') which could be earned in the revenue–sharing sector. We might typify this as a national wage bargain which laid down a minimum wage rate of w'' for all fixed–wage concerns but required all revenue–sharing enterprises to be organized on the basis of a rigidly fixed wage w together with a rigidly fixed share s, w and s being calculated to produce an inclusive rate of pay equivalent to the w'' prescribed for fixed–wage firms.

In this section we relax these conditions by dropping the requirement that each revenue–sharing firm pays a rigidly fixed w and a rigidly fixed s, and allowing it to choose from time to time any combination of w and s which will result in an inclusive rate of pay at least as high as the prescribed minimum w'' set for the fixed–wage firms. It will now be possible for revenue–sharing firms to survive in competition with fixed–wage firms.

In order to analyse the situation where w and s are in this sense fully flexible, we differentiate the expression for the inclusive rate of pay of an individual firm from (V.b.17), namely:

$$w' = \bar{w} + \frac{\bar{s}x\bar{p}}{l} \qquad \text{(V.f.1)}$$

keeping w' constant, which gives

$$\bar{l}\,\mathrm{d}\bar{w} + \bar{x}\bar{p}\,\mathrm{d}\bar{s} = \{\bar{w}' - \bar{w} - \bar{s}\bar{\lambda}\}\,\mathrm{d}\bar{l} - \bar{s}\bar{x}\,\mathrm{d}\bar{k}, \qquad \text{(V.f.2)}$$

where $\bar{w}' - \bar{w} = \bar{s}\bar{x}\bar{p}/\bar{l}$ and $\lambda = (\bar{x}\bar{p}/\bar{l})(\beta/[1+\bar{\pi}])$ in conditions both of unemployment and of full employment.

Rearranging (V.f.2) we obtain

$$\bar{l}\,\delta\bar{w}' = \bar{s}\bar{\lambda}\,\frac{1+\bar{\pi}-\beta}{\beta}\,\mathrm{d}\bar{l} - \bar{s}\bar{x}\,\mathrm{d}\bar{k}, \qquad \text{(V.f.3)}$$

where

$$\delta\bar{w}' = \mathrm{d}\bar{w} + \frac{\bar{x}\bar{p}}{\bar{l}}\,\mathrm{d}\bar{s}$$

or the increase in the inclusive rate of pay that would result from an increase in the pay parameters w and s if $\bar{x}\bar{p}/\bar{l}$ were unchanged.

We can interpret this result in the following way. Consider an employer with a constant capital stock ($\mathrm{d}\bar{k} = 0$) who raises his pay offer by $\delta\bar{w}'$. From (V.f.3) we see that he will attract an amount of additional labour equal to

$$\mathrm{d}\bar{l} = \frac{\beta\bar{l}}{\bar{s}\bar{\lambda}(1+\bar{\pi}-\beta)}\,\delta\bar{w}'. \qquad \text{(V.f.4)}$$

As the improved pay offer attracts more labour, revenue per head ($\bar{x}\bar{p}/\bar{l}$) will fall both because output per head will fall (cf. II.c.5), and also because the selling price will have to be reduced in order to market the larger output. Thus the share element ($\bar{s}\bar{x}\bar{p}/\bar{l}$) in the firm's inclusive rate of pay will fall and the inclusive rate of pay will once more be reduced. This will go on until the inclusive rate of pay which had been raised by $\delta\bar{w}'$ is reduced to its original level, and the necessary increase in employment needed for this result is given in (V.f.4).

Or consider an employer which with a constant labour force ($\mathrm{d}\bar{l} = 0$) is undertaking a capital investment programme of $\mathrm{d}\bar{k}$. The increased capital will increase total revenue by its marginal revenue product (x). This increase will raise total revenue per worker $\bar{x}\bar{p}/\bar{l}$ and will thus raise the share element in the inclusive rate of pay $\bar{s}\bar{x}\bar{p}/\bar{l}$. If the employer does not want to attract more labour, he can reduce his pay parameters s and w so as to offset the increase in the pay which would otherwise occur. From (V.f.3) we can see that the resulting possible reduction in his pay offer is given by

$$\delta \bar{w}' = -\frac{\bar{s}\bar{x}}{\bar{l}}\, \mathrm{d}\bar{k}\,. \qquad \text{(V.f.5)}$$

If we suppose that the employer can make these flexible adjustments in the way described above, he can act as if he were simply paying a fixed wage rate equal to w', since he can now take on more or less labour at this rate by appropriate adjustments in s or w as revenue per head varies and adjustment is needed to keep inclusive pay equal to w'.

The employer will now have an incentive, by making the necessary adjustments to his pay parameters s and w, to take on more or less labour according as the marginal revenue product is greater or less than the rate of pay, w', i.e. according as $\bar{\lambda} \gtrless w'$ as given in the previous section in (V.e.2).[1]

Moreover if w' is kept constant in this manner, the cost of taking on one more unit of capital will be equated to h'', the outside market hire of capital. Without such adjustment the cost of taking on one more unit of capital is $h'' + \bar{s}\bar{x}$ since a proportion ($\bar{s}$) of the capital's marginal revenue product ($\bar{x}$) must be paid to labour in addition to the market cost of the capital itself (h''). But with flexible pay parameters this can be offset by the reduction in parameters of pay to labour which can be made to offset the rise in the share element of their pay and this reduction, ($\bar{l}\, \delta \bar{w}'$), as can be seen from (V.f.3), is equal to $\bar{s}\bar{x}$, so that the net cost of a unit of capital is

$$h'' + \bar{s}\bar{x} - \bar{s}\bar{x} = h''. \qquad \text{(V.f.6)}$$

Thus an employer will have an incentive to employ more capital so long as

$$\bar{x} > h''$$

as given in the previous section is (V.e.2).

[1] The process by which flexible pay parameters are adjusted so as to bring the rate of pay into line with labour's marginal revenue product is illustrated geometrically for a Pure Share Economy in the Note at the end of this section.

It is, however, important to note that the incentive to invest up to the point at which x has fallen to h'' will hold good only so long as the pay parameters are not merely fully flexible, but are confidently expected to be fully flexible, by the employer concerned. He will calculate on the basis that he will gain the full marginal revenue product from an investment only if he feels sure that any increase in revenue per worker which it brings about will in fact be offset by an offsetting downward adjustment of his pay parameters.

In the resulting equilibrium with the firm's inclusive rate of pay (w') equal to the outside fixed rate of pay (w'') and also to labour's marginal revenue product (λ) we would have for each firm

$$w'' = w + \frac{sxp}{l} = \lambda = \frac{xp}{l}\frac{\beta}{1+\pi}$$

or V.f.7

$$w'' = \frac{w\beta}{\beta - s(1+\pi)},$$

which expresses the relation between s and w which, given β and π, is needed to maintain equilibrium.

A very similar analysis applies in the profit–sharing regime.

Instead of (V.f.1) we have

$$w' = \bar{w} + \frac{\bar{s}(\bar{x}\bar{p} - \bar{w}\bar{l} - h\bar{k})}{\bar{l}}, \qquad \text{V.f.8}$$

which instead of (V.f.2) gives

$$\bar{l}\left\{d\bar{w} + \frac{\bar{x}\bar{p} - \bar{w}\bar{l} - h\bar{k}}{\bar{l}}\,d\bar{s}\right\} = \{\bar{w}' - (1-s)\bar{w} - \bar{s}\bar{\lambda}\}\,d\bar{l} - \bar{s}(\bar{x} - h)\,d\bar{k}$$

V.f.9

with $$h'' = \frac{1-\bar{s}}{1-\phi\bar{s}}\,\bar{x}$$

so that $$\bar{x} - h = \frac{1-\phi}{1-\phi s}\,\bar{x}$$

and with $$w' - (1-\bar{s})\bar{w} - \bar{s}\bar{\lambda} = \bar{s}\left(\frac{\bar{x}\bar{p} - h\bar{k}}{\bar{l}} - \bar{\lambda}\right),$$

which, after use of equations (II.c.15 and V.b.14 and 15), gives

$$w' - (1 - \bar{s})\bar{w} - \bar{s}\bar{\lambda} = \bar{s}\bar{\lambda}\,\frac{1 + \bar{\pi} - \beta - \alpha\phi(1 - \bar{s})/(1 - \phi\bar{s})}{\beta} \qquad \text{V.f.10}$$

Re–arrangement of (V.f.9) then gives instead of (V.f.3)

$$\bar{l}\,\delta\bar{w}' = \bar{s}\bar{\lambda}\,\frac{1 + \bar{\pi} - \beta - \alpha\phi(1 - \bar{s})/(1 - \phi\bar{s})}{\beta}\,\mathrm{d}\bar{l} - \bar{s}\,\frac{1 - \phi}{1 - \phi\bar{s}}\,\bar{x}\,\mathrm{d}\bar{k} \qquad \text{V.f.11}$$

with corresponding adjustments to equations (V.f.4, 5 and 6).

The equilibrium relationship between s and w is then given by

$$w'' = \frac{w\beta}{\beta - s(1 + \pi)}(1 - s)\left(1 - \frac{s\alpha\phi}{1 - \phi s}\right) \qquad \text{V.f.12}$$

in place of (V.f.7).

In both cases of revenue sharing and profit sharing the increased competition for capital funds to increase investment would mean that the monetary authorities would have to raise the hire–charge for capital up to the level of $h'' = x = (Y/K^*)(\alpha/[1 + \pi])$. The pay of labour would remain at the outside fixed rate of w'' if w'' had been set at a rate higher than the full–employment marginal product of labour, namely $(Y/L^*)(\beta/[1 + \pi])$. If it had been set below this level, the competition between the individual employers as they raised their pay parameters s and w so as to attract more labour so long as $w' < \lambda^*$ would raise the outside competitive rate of pay up to the full employment value of labour's marginal revenue product $(Y/L^*)(\beta/[1 + \pi])$.

The implication of these results is that if the parameters w and s are in this way fully flexible by the individual firm, then the individual share–economy firm will have an incentive (1) to employ labour up to the point at which the worker's marginal revenue product is equal to the ruling inclusive rate of pay and (2), provided that the full flexibility of the parameters s and w is confidently expected to operate in the future, to invest in capital up to the point at which the marginal revenue product of capital is equal to the ruling market hire–charge for capital (h''). The individual share–economy firm will then be behaving exactly like an individual fixed–wage firm except for the fact that at every point of time, with any particular set of s and w parameters ruling in the current pay contract, it will be anxious to take on more labour.

In the case of the revenue–sharing firm this is so because with the inclusive rate of pay equal to labour's marginal revenue product $((xp/l)(\beta/[1+\pi]))$ we have

$$w' = w + \frac{sxp}{l} = \frac{xp}{l}\frac{\beta}{1+\pi}, \qquad \text{(V.f.13)}$$

which gives

$$w = \frac{xp}{l}\frac{\beta}{1+\pi}\left(1 - s\frac{1+\pi}{\beta}\right) < \frac{xp}{l}\frac{\beta}{1+\pi}(1-s), \qquad \text{(V.f.14)}$$

so that from (V.b.3) it can be seen that at constant parameters s and w employers would wish to increase employment.

In the case of the profit–sharing firm we would have

$$w' = w + \frac{s(xp - wl - hk)}{l} = \frac{xp}{l}\frac{\beta}{1+\pi}, \qquad \text{(V.f.15)}$$

which implies

$$w < \frac{xp}{l}\frac{\beta}{1+\pi} \text{ if } q_a > 0 \qquad \text{(V.f.16)}$$

so that from (V.b.9) it can be seen that at constant pay parameters the employer would seek to employ more labour if the accounting profit was positive.

Thus, although as we have seen in this section it would not pay the employer to raise either the s or the w in order to attract more labour, the employer would in these conditions always welcome more labour at the given pay parameters. However if he did succeed temporarily in taking on more labour at the ruling pay parameters, this would in fact lead to a fall in w' below its currently ruling level. He would, therefore, quickly lose any extra labour which he did manage temporarily to attract.

Thus in these conditions a share economy firm with fully flexible pay parameters would always welcome more labour if it could obtain it at the current rates of s and w, and it would at the same time survive competition from fixed–wage firms. Indeed, in all other relevant respects it would behave like a fixed–wage firm. But this conclusion rests upon the assumption that the individual firm is fully free, and is fully confident that it will remain fully free, to adjust the levels of s and w which it is offering to its workforce in any way that it chooses, provided that the inclusive rate of pay which results does not fall below the prescribed minimum w'' or any higher level of w' which may be set through its competition with other firms.

Note to Section (f) of Chapter V on a Geometrical Illustration of the Adjustment of a Flexible s Parameter in a Pure Share Economy

Consider a single firm with an average revenue product of labour (ARP) and a marginal revenue product (MRP) as in Figure V.f.1., faced by a fixed wage rate (o*w*). Employment will be equal to wd where wage rate = MRP. Suppose now that it abolishes the fixed wage altogether and offers a share equal to os in the revenue (value-added) of the firm. Then its offer of pay per unit of labour or average labour income (ALI) is given by the line sp and the marginal labour income (MLI). by the line sq. (The ALI is o*s*/o*r* × ARP and the MLI is o*s*/o*r* × MRP because for both average and marginal revenue a fraction o*s*/o*r* must be paid in income to labour). It is to be noted that the average income to the worker (ALI) is the same as the average cost of labour to the employer (ALC) and similarly the marginal payments represent income to the worker and cost to the employer (MLI = MLC).

With the worker's share equal to o*s*/o*r* employment will be wa because labour will be attracted up to the point at which ALC falls to the competitive rate of pay o*w*. The employer will want to take on labour up to o*q*, i.e. so long as the MRP > 0, because he will get his share of any additional revenue. In Figure 1 at employment *wa* (the maximum that the employer can attract at the given wage share o*s*/o*r*) the MRP of labour at *b* remains greater than the MLC at c, so there remains an excess demand for labour.

But the employer will have an incentive to reduce the share offered to labour so long as the ALC is above the MRP (i.e. so long as the point *a* is above the point *b*). When the share has been reduced from o*s*/o*r* to o*s*'/o*r* the amount of labour offering its services will have fallen from *wa* to *wd*. At this point ALC = MRP. The employer will have reduced his purchase of labour by *da* **at what is in effect the constant price** o*w* and will thus have added the triangle *abd* to his net revenue by dismissing all labour for which the MRP was below the **constant price** o*w*. Nevertheless when the point *d* is reached the employer will still want to employ more labour if any should present itself to him, because the MLC at *e* is below the MRP at *d*.

For this reason if the parameter o*s*/o*r* is fully flexible, equilibrium will be found in the share economy at exactly the same point *d* as in the fixed–wage economy; but in the former case employers will all the time be trying to extend employment (because that means an automatic fall in the ALC), whereas in the latter case they will have no such incentive (because the ALC is fixed at o*w*).

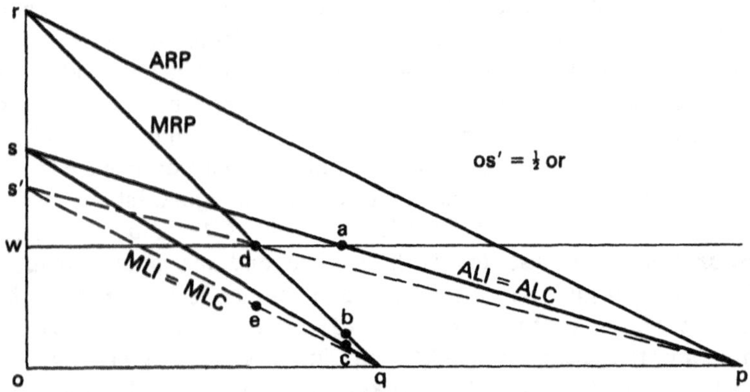

Figure V.f.1

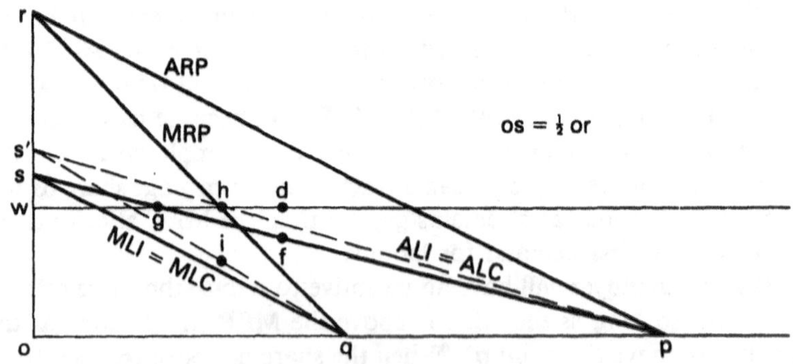

Figure V.f.2

Figure V.f.1 is so drawn that the final equilibrium share going to labour is (*os*′/*or*) is ½. We start with an unchanged pay contract in Figure V.f.2. where *os*/*or* is ½. But the ARP has been shifted to the left to represent a fall in demand for the firm's product, the outside competitive rate of pay remaining unchanged at o*w*. With the existing share pay contract the effect of the reduction in the ARP and so automatically in the ALC will be a reduction not, as in the wage economy, in employment from *d* to *h* but in the rate of pay from *d* to *f*, where *wd* is the same length in both Figures. Labour will not be unemployed. If other firms are also share–economy firms and have suffered in the same way, the competitive rate of pay will also have fallen from *d* to *f* and that is the end of the story. If the fall in demand is confined to this firm, there will not be unemployment; but workers will be tempted away to employment in other firms so long as the ALI is below o*w*, so that employment in this firm will be reduced from *d* towards *g*. But at *g* the MRP would be above o*w* and the employer will now have an incentive to raise the wage share he offers from *os*/*or* to *os*′/*or* and thus to stabilize employment at *h* where MRP = ALC. As before, at this point the employer will have an incentive to seek out any workers who will join his workforce at the given share *os*′/*or* since the MRP at h is greater than the MLC at *i*; but he will not have any incentive to raise the ratio *os*′/*or* still further as a means of attracting such workers.

(g) Full Employment through Full Flexibility

In Sections (a), (b) and (c) of this chapter we assumed that all firms had to pay fixed–wage rates of *w* plus a share (*s*) of the firm's revenue. In Section (e) we relaxed this by assuming that firms could switch over to a wholly fixed–wage regime provided they paid at least as much as a prescribed minimum wage rate. In Section (f) we introduced the further relaxation that revenue–sharing firms could choose what values they chose for *s* and *w* provided they too paid at least as much as the prescribed minimum in their inclusive rate of pay.

As we saw in Section (f) of this chapter competition among employers will serve, if necessary, to bring the ruling rate of inclusive pay up to the value of full–employment marginal product of labour (λ^*). If we now add downward flexibility to any prescribed minimum by assuming that the competition of unemployed workers will bring the minimum down so long as it is above the full–employment marginal revenue product of labour (λ^*), we will end up with the same results as in the full–employment situations in a Capitalist Wage Economy. If the number of firms is given exogenously the economy will be in the same basic situation as in Section (d) of Chapter III; if the number of firms increases until $q = 0$ the economy will be in the same basic situation as in Section (e) of Chapter III.

There would, however, remain one distinctive feature of a revenue–sharing economy. At any one time at any given values of s and w agreed between employer and employees the employer will always be willing to employ more workers. The employer will not be prepared to raise s and/or w in order to attract more workers, but he will increase his profit if he can attract any additional employees at these rates, even though the marginal revenue product of labour is already reduced to equality with the inclusive rate of pay which his workers are receiving.

(h) Concluding Observations on the Capitalist Share Economy

From the analysis of the preceding sections of this chapter we have drawn the conclusion that a Capitalist Share Economy is an effective method of organization only if the pay parameters s and w are fully flexible. This conclusion is, however, not valid in one extreme case, namely that of the Pure Profit–Sharing Economy where the fixed–wage element in pay (w) is set at the full value of the outside market rate of pay (w'') and the fixed–interest element (h) is set at the full value of the outside market hire-charge (h''). In this case the arrangement is simply one in which any monopolistic profit or loss is shared in the ratio $s:(1-s)$ between labour and capital. This may be a good arrangement for purposes of improving work incentives and industrial relations. It does so, moreover, in a way which does not prevent both labour and capital from being employed up to the point at which their marginal revenue product has fallen to equality with their outside market price, since the capitalist employer will always receive his share $(1-s)$ of any excess of the marginal revenue product over market cost of the factor.

But in this case in equilibrium the employer will not have any excess demand for labour at the ruling parameters, w and s, since in equilibrium an additional worker would receive the whole of his marginal revenue product and there would be no extra revenue to the capitalist resulting from his employment. In other cases of the Capitalist Share Economy in equilibrium with fully flexible pay parameters there would always remain some excess demand for labour at the current ruling pay parameters, as we have seen in Section (f). It is just this feature which gives a very special character to share–economy arrangements. It means that, so long as the currently contracted pay parameters persist, the impact effect of a decline in demand will in the first place be merely to reduce the excess in the demand for labour and, only after the reduction of demand has passed a certain critical point, will it begin to cause any reduction in the scale of employment.

Theoretically it would be possible to devise a profit–sharing arrangement which shared between capitalists and workers an accounting profit which took the form of the firm's revenue after deduction of a fixed–wage element which was markedly less than the outside market rate of earnings ($wl < w''l$) but after deduction of the full market charge for capital ($hk = h''k$). In this case there would be no danger of a disincentive to investment, since the capitalist employer would always receive his share $(1 - s)$ of any excess of an investment's marginal revenue product over its market cost. At the same time at the currently existing low fixed wage there would be an excess demand for labour.

But any such arrangement would be manifestly unfair. It would mean that capital always received its full market charge plus an additional sum equal to $(1 - s)/s$ times the share element in labour's pay. It would presumably be impossible to envisage an arrangement whereby the whole of the ruling market charge for capital was excluded from the shareable accounting profit unless the whole of the ruling market pay for labour was also so deducted. In other words if we are to consider cases in which there will remain an excess demand for labour, we must also consider at the same time that, if the currently ruling pay parameters were not confidently expected to be fully flexible in the future, capital investment would expect a reward less than its marginal revenue product.

The combined existence of these features is illustrated most easily in the case of revenue–sharing arrangements and since it is on these features that we wish to comment we will illustrate the points in what follows with reference only to revenue–sharing arrangements.

It is clear from the preceding sections of this chapter that if Capitalist–Revenue–Sharing Firms are to survive in competition with Capitalist Wage Firms either or both of the two pay parameters s and w must be flexible. This requirement is particularly important in its effect upon the incentives of a firm to invest in capital equipment. If the pay parameters were rigidly fixed with $s > 0$, a firm which invested in new capital equipment would have to surrender a proportion s of the resulting additional value of its production to the wage earners. Either this would discourage the capital investment or else the authorities would have to reduce the market rate of return on capital funds to make the cost of installing the new capital that much easier; but in the latter case fixed–wage firms which did not need to surrender any part of the additional value of their product to their workers would be in a more favourable position than their revenue–sharing competitors.

This disadvantage to the revenue–sharing firms would disappear if when the additional revenue matured from the additional investment, it were possible for the managers of the firms concerned to reduce the pay parameters s and/or w below what they would otherwise have been to the extent necessary to offset the otherwise fortuitous gain to the workers; but this would, of course, remove the reluctance of the revenue–sharing firm to invest only if, when the decision to invest was taken, reliance could confidently be put upon this future flexibility of the pay parameters.

Moreover the necessary downward flexibility would have to be one which resulted from an individual bargain between the particular firm concerned and its own employees. The disincentive to investment would not be removed unless a firm which decided to make an additional capital investment could expect to enjoy a reduction of its pay parameters relative to those payable by a firm which was not carrying out an investment programme. What is needed, therefore, is a state of effective competition in the labour market between one firm and another, so that a firm which carried out an investment programme would not need to allow its inclusive rate of pay to rise above that offered by any competitors who were not investing; this would mean that it could make the reductions in its own pay parameters to the extent needed to avoid the rise which would otherwise take place. For this to be the case the pay parameters s and w must not be the subject of an industry–wide pay bargain between a confederation of employers and an industry–wide trade union, though the inclusive rate of pay w' could be fixed for the industry without inhibiting capital investment by an individual firm.

Any persistent inflexibility or stickiness of the pay parameters could also cause a severe conflict of interest between employers and employees. For the reasons set out at length in this chapter any stickiness of the pay parameters would increase the incentive of employers to expand employment beyond the level which would be profitable in a fixed–wage firm, but would reduce their incentive to invest in capital equipment. But the same stickiness of the pay parameters would have exactly the opposite effect on the attitude of the workers. They would be in favour of any investment plan that would add anything however small to the value of the firm's output, since they would automatically receive their share of that addition. On the other hand, the existing workers would be restrictive in their attitudes towards proposals to expand the workforce beyond the point at which the value of output per head was maximized, because some part of each worker's pay took the form of a share of that maximized value. Thus any rigidity or stickiness in the pay parameters would be likely to increase the desire of the workers to participate in managerial decisions about output and investment and indeed to exacerbate the grounds for conflict about such decisions.

There is one further problem which would arise in the real world if there were any undue rigidity or stickiness in the shares of the firm's revenue which were allocated to labour and capital. In the simple model used in this book all firms are assumed to be alike. But, in the real world, in some lines of activity firms will be much more labour intensive than in others. Thus the share going to labour (s) will be much higher in a labour–intensive firm than in a capital–intensive firm; and this will also be the case in a Partial Revenue–Sharing Economy if more or less the same proportion of inclusive rates of pay takes the form of a share (s) rather than a fixed wage (w) in all types of business. Thus the disincentive to investment due to the fact that a pre–determined share of any consequential increase in revenue must be paid to labour will be very much greater for labour–intensive than for capital–intensive firms. It will still be possible for the financial authorities by reducing the rate of interest to induce businesses as a whole to invest in the given 'target' amount of real capital (K^*); but this will be at the expense of a relative extra incentive to capital–intensive firms at the expense of labour–intensive firms.

A similar problem would arise in connection with foreign investment. If capital movements from the country in question were uncontrolled, and if there were no special tax on such capital funds or on the yield on such capital funds as were invested abroad, there would be a powerful incentive to invest abroad, where there was no requirement to share the yield with labour, rather than invest at home. Some sort of equalizing tax would probably be found necessary to close the gap between foreign rates of interest and the home rate of interest after it had been reduced sufficiently to offset the share of the yield on home investment which was allocated to labour.

So much for the potential dangers of a revenue–sharing system which would arise if there were any appreciable fixity or stickiness in a firm's pay parameters. There stands on the other side of the account one great advantage which could be gained from such a system if reliance could be placed on sufficient long–run flexibility in the pay parameters. At any one time, in the short run, wage contracts would be set in terms of the parameters s and w; and as we have seen in Section (f) of this chapter, employers, although unwilling to raise these parameters, would nevertheless be anxious to take into employment any additional workers who came forward for employment at these parameters. In this sense there would be a perpetual short–run excess demand for labour; and this fact could have a most important and beneficial effect on the way in which fluctuations in total demand would exert their influence.

We may illustrate the importance of this effect by considering a revenue–sharing economy which starts in the full–employment situation described in Section (g) of this chapter with full long–run flexibility of its pay parameters s and w. Suppose that there were then an unexpected fall in the level of total demand so that Y fell from Y_1 to Y_2 without any simultaneous change in the parameters w and s.

In the initial situation with confident expectation of long–run flexibility of the parameters s and w we would start with both

$$w_1' = w + \frac{sY_1}{L^*} \text{ and } w_1' = \lambda_1^* = \frac{Y_1}{L^*}\frac{\beta}{1+\pi}, \qquad \text{V.h.1}$$

which implies that the fixed–wage element in pay is

$$w = \frac{Y_1}{L^*}\left(\frac{\beta}{1+\pi} - s\right). \qquad \text{V.h.2}$$

The meaning of this equation is clear. $(Y_1/L^*)(\beta/[1+\pi])$ is the marginal revenue product of labour which is equal to the inclusive rate of pay w_1'; sY_1/L^* is the share element in w_1, so that the fixed–wage element (w) must make up the difference.

But as we know from (V.b.6), at unchanged parameters s and w, there will remain an excess demand for labour after the fall of Y_1 to Y_2, provided that

$$w < \frac{Y_2}{L^*}\frac{\beta(1-s)}{1+\pi} \qquad \text{V.h.3}$$

that is to say, using (V.h.2), provided that

$$\frac{Y_2}{Y_1} > \frac{1-\dfrac{s(1+\pi)}{\beta}}{1-s} \qquad \text{V.h.4}$$

We know from (V.h.2) that as s ranges from 0 to $\beta/(1+\pi)$ with w ranging at the same time from λ_1^*, to 0, so $s(1+\pi)/\beta$ ranges from 0 to 1 with the lower limit to Y_2/Y_1 set by (V.h.4) at a positive fraction ranging from 1 to 0.

Thus so long as the fall in Y is confined within the limit set by (V.h.4), the immediate reaction of producers to a fall in demand would be to cut prices and profits rather than output and employment.

The fall in Y will, of course, have reduced the marginal revenue product of labour from

$$\lambda_1^*, = (Y_1/L^*)(\beta/[1+\pi]) \text{ to } \lambda_2^* = (Y_2/L^*)(\beta/[1+\pi]);$$

and it will also have reduced the inclusive rate of pay of the worker from

$$w_1' = w + \frac{sY_1}{L^*}$$

to

$$w_2' = w + \frac{sY_2}{L^*}$$

The reduction in λ^* will be

$$\lambda_1^* - \lambda_2^* = \frac{\beta}{L^*(1+\pi)}(Y_1 - Y_2) \qquad \text{V.h.5}$$

and in w' will be

$$w_1' - w_2' = \frac{s}{L^*}(Y_1 - Y_2) \qquad \text{V.h.6}$$

so that

$$\frac{w_1' - w_2'}{\lambda_1^* - \lambda_2^*} = \frac{s(1+\pi)}{\beta}. \qquad \text{V.h.7}$$

But from (V.h.2) we know that according as $w \geqslant 0$, so $s(1+\pi)/\beta \leqslant 1$. It follows from (V.h.7) that, starting with $w_1' = \lambda_1^*$, w' will fall by the same amount as λ^* in a pure share economy (i.e. with $w = 0$), but will fall less than λ^* in a revenue–sharing firm with $w > 0$. In this latter case we would have $w_2' > \lambda_2^*$.

In this situation with flexibility of the parameters s and w individual employers would reduce their offer of s and/or w in any renewed wage contracts until w_2' was equal to λ_2^*.

Thus in these circumstances with full flexibility the immediate response of employers to a fall in Y would be to cut their prices rather than their outputs and subsequently to take action to restore their profit through a reduction in their wage costs s and w.

In a Capitalist Wage Economy the response of employers to a fall in demand would be in the opposite order. At any given fixed–wage rate the immediate response of employers would be to reduce output and employment. It would be only at a later date that, if there were sufficient flexibility of the fixed wage, the cost of labour might be reduced and employment restored.

This is the basic claim in favour of a Capitalist Revenue–Sharing organization; and it would indeed be no small benefit to society that fluctuations in demand should in the first instance affect prices and profits rather than output and employment and that subsequent adjustments of wage rates should be needed to restore profits rather than to restore outputs. The real losses due to the waste of the unemployed resources would be avoided. Flexibility of the pay parameters s and w is, however, a necessary condition for this benefit to be realized.

Throughout this chapter we have ignored one other possible beneficial effect of a revenue–sharing or profit–sharing organization. In the precise mechanical models which we have constructed we have paid no attention to the possible beneficial effects on workers' incentives to work efficiently which might result from the fact that they will automatically gain a share of any increase in the firm's total revenue which may result from their increased effort. The system might in fact improve the firm's production function. Any such gain would in reality need to be balanced against the potential dangers mentioned earlier in this section. It will, however, be our task in the next chapter to design a somewhat modified type of share economy which will preserve the advantages of such an organization with less danger from its possible damaging features.

CHAPTER VI

Discriminating Labour–Capital Partnerships

(a) The Objectives of Discriminating Labour–Capital Partnerships

An attempt is made in this final chapter to design an institutional set–up for an enterprise with the following characteristics.

1. It makes the income of the workers depend in whole or part on the success of the enterprise as in the cases of the Non–Discriminating Labour Co–operatives and the Capitalist Sharing Firms analysed in Chapters IV and V. It thus preserves any beneficial effects on incentives which may result from this principle.
2. It avoids the dangers that may arise in a Capitalist Sharing Firm from undue rigidity or stickiness of the shares of the firm's revenue which may be allotted to labour and to capital. The proposed institutional set–up achieves the appropriate flexibility through an automatic inbuilt adjustment of these shares.
3. It thus removes the large element of direct conflict of interest between labour and capital which, as we saw in Section (h) of Chapter V, can arise from share rigidities; and in this way it makes it easier to arrange for labour's participation with capital in decision–making about the firm's plans for investment and employment.
4. It avoids the instabilities which were found in Chapter IV to be a feature of Non–Discriminating Labour Co–operatives.
5. It mitigates the undue reliance on ease of entry and exit of firms into and out of the market which was also found in Chapter IV to be a feature of Non–Discriminating Labour Co–operatives.
6. It avoids also the undue concentration of risk which we also saw in Chapter IV as a possible result of a Non–Discriminating Labour Co–operative, particularly if it were set up in a capital–intensive type of activity.
7. It has as favourable an effect on the stability of employment and a more favourable effect upon the levels of employment that might result from Capitalist Sharing arrangements.

These are far–reaching claims. As will be explained below their attainment depends upon the abandonment of any rigid application of the principle of equal income for equal work. 'New hands' from outside must not immediately claim full participation in the profits of a successful enterprise which are being enjoyed by the existing insiders or 'old hands' who have been responsible for building up that success. As we have seen in Chapter IV, it is the rigid application of the principles of non–discrimination which flaws the operation of Non–Discriminating Labour Co–operatives.

But, alas, it is not possible in this wicked world to devise any flawless arrangements. In addition to the question how far the abandonment of the strict principle of 'equal pay for equal work' could be made acceptable (see Section (g)), it is not possible to remove all conflicts of interest between labour and capital (see Section(e)) and, in particular, it is not possible to provide the needed job security for the worker members of a partnership without imposing some extra risk or cost on investment and technological innovation by the members who provide the capital (see Section (d)).

(b) Outline of a Pure Discriminating Labour–Capital Partnership

In fact as we will show in the next section of this chapter, the principle of Labour–Capital Partnership can be introduced partially into an enterprise on as large or small a scale as the capitalists and workers in the concern may agree to be desirable, just as the sharing principle discussed in Chapter V can be introduced in a large or small measure according as the emphasis is placed on the pay parameter s or on the pay parameter w in the make–up of inclusive pay. But it will be easier to introduce the principle and to discuss its basic merits and demerits in the pure form in which the whole of the income of the firm is distributed on a labour–capital partnership principle.

Consider a Capitalist Wage Firm of the kind discussed in Chapter III. Suppose that of its revenue (xp) 80 per cent is being paid to the employees (wl) and the remaining 20 per cent ($hk + q$) is accruing to the capitalists. Simple conversion of this into a pure Labour–Capital Partnership would consist of the issue of two kinds of Share Certificates namely: (1) Capital Share Certificates which would be distributed to all the persons who were in fact receiving directly or indirectly through profit interest, rent etc, the capitalists' 20 per cent share of the firm's revenue, this distribution to each beneficiary being *pro rata* to his or her existing income from the business; and (2) Labour Share Certificates which would be distributed to all employees *pro rata* to their individual earnings of the remaining 80 per cent of the firm's revenue.

All Share Certificates, whether Capital or Labour, would carry an entitlement to the same rate of dividend.

The immediate result of this conversion would be that everyone concerned would receive an unchanged income, but in every case in the form of a dividend on a shareholding, which would replace all interest, rent, wages etc.; but everyone concerned in the operation of the business would now have a share in the future success or failure of the enterprise.

There would, however, be one basic distinction between Capital Share Certificates and Labour Share Certificates.

Capital Share Certificates would correspond more or less exactly to a company's existing Ordinary Shares. They could be freely traded on the Stock Exchange or elsewhere in the market and could be transferred from one owner to another.

Labour Share Certificates on the other hand would be tied to the individual employee and would be surrendered and cancelled when the employee retired or voluntarily left the business. They would not, however, be cancelled if the employee left the firm involuntarily (e.g. because of redundancy), unless the dismissal was due to grave misconduct or illness which incapacitated the worker for his job. The worker would thus normally be guaranteed his employment, or at least his appropriate share of income from employment, until retirement. His claim on the firm would however be tied to his availability to perform the work for which the dividend on Labour Share Certificates was the reward. There could, of course, as now be separate pension arrangements for those who had retired, together with separate arrangements for the support of worker partners in ill health.

Proposals for the issue of Labour Share Certificates of the kind suggested in this chapter are to be clearly distinguished from schemes designed to endow workers with ordinary shares in the firms which employ them. Such schemes are often known as Employee Share Ownership Plans.

A typical scheme of this kind may take the following form. The company rewards its employees in part by payments into a trust fund.

This fund then uses the money to purchase the company's shares and either holds them on trust for the benefit of the present and future employees of the company or distributes them among the individual employees to be held by them on their own personal accounts. We will consider only the latter case in order to make the closest possible comparison with our present partnership proposals. Under such an Employee Share Ownership Plan the individual employee will be required to hold his allotment of the company's ordinary shares either for a specified period of time or alternatively until he leaves the firm on retirement or otherwise, at which point he will be free to sell his shares – or indeed may be required to do so. Thus shares become available again in the market for purchase by the trust fund for allotment to newly employed workers. Any voting rights and the financial return on the shares so held give the employees an extra interest in the conduct and fortunes of the firm.

Such schemes for employee ownership of the firm's ordinary shares differ in two basic respects from the issue of Labour Share Certificates under the proposed partnership arrangements. In the first place, such schemes promote worker participation in the firm's fortunes only in so far as a part of the worker's past pay has taken the form of compulsory savings (similar to compulsory contributions to a firm's pension fund) rather than the receipt of freely disposable income, whereas Labour Share Certificates depend directly upon the employee's current supply of work and effort to the firm without any reference to past compulsory savings. In the second place, such schemes imply that employees should put their eggs in one basket by investing their capital (in so far as it results from the accumulation of these past compulsory savings) in the same concern to which they have committed their prospects of employment, whereas with Labour Share Certificates workers remain perfectly free to commit all their financial wealth to other risks in other concerns, and would indeed be wise to do so. The distinction between Capital and Labour Share Certificates enables each factor to enjoy the advantages and to accept the responsibilities of partnership simply in respect to that resource (whether capital funds or labour effort) which in the nature of things it must commit to the firm's use and for the period for which it makes that commitment.

With these arrangements major decisions about changes in the scale of employment or of capital investment could be taken in such a way that any action would be to the advantage of all shareholders, whether capitalists or workers, since, if a high dividend is to result, it will result for all owners and all employees.

An existing worker would be free to leave if he could earn elsewhere a higher pay than his expected dividend income from the firm. The management of the firm would be free to offer him an issue of additional Labour Share Certificates sufficient to persuade him to stay, if they thought that the marginal revenue product of the worker in question (i.e. what would be lost to the revenue of the firm if the worker concerned did leave the firm) was higher than the enlarged dividend income on his enlarged holding of Labour Share Certificates; and in this case all existing shareholders would gain from his retention because they would thereby avoid a reduction in the revenue from which share dividends had to be financed which would have been greater than the saving of dividends payable to the retained worker.

In an exactly similar manner the managers of the firm would be free to decide to take on an additional worker by offering to him or her a new issue of Labour Share Certificates which was sufficient to attract the worker to the enterprise; if the expected dividend on these shares, while sufficient to attract the worker, was nevertheless lower than the expected marginal revenue product of the new worker, all existing shareholders, whether capitalist or worker, would stand to gain by the decision, since the addition to the firm's revenue available to be paid out in increased dividends on all shares of both kinds would be greater than the additional dividend payable to the new worker on the newly issued Share Certificates. Since the new worker would presumably be attracted only if there was some advantage to him in accepting the offer, everyone would gain from such a decision.

Exactly the same considerations would be relevant for decisions to invest in more capital equipment. The purchase of a new machine could be financed by issuing and selling on the market an issue of additional Capital Share Certificates sufficient to raise the necessary funds. All existing shareholders, whether Capital or Labour Shareholders, would gain if the dividend payable on the new additional Capital Share Certificates was less than the addition which the new capital equipment would add to the firm's revenue (i.e. less than the marginal revenue product of the capital equipment). Thus the answer to a question whether to carry out an investment plan would depend upon a judgement whether it was to the advantage or disadvantage of all persons, whether capitalists or workers who were concerned with the firm's activities.

Thus if one compares the structural arrangements of a Pure Labour–Capital Partnership with those of a Pure Share Economy Firm, one outstanding feature is that the former provides automatically the required flexibility of the share–ratio in which the revenue is divided between capital and labour, the possible absence of which can so seriously flaw the workings of the latter. For example, the danger that investment in capital equipment will be held up in the Share Economy because a proportion s of the marginal revenue product of the new capital would accrue to the workers, unless the ratio s were sufficiently flexible downwards, is avoided in the Labour–Capital Partnership Firm because the issue of additional Capital Share Certificates to finance the new investment results automatically in the appropriate increase in the share of the revenue accruing to capital.

(c) Partial Discriminating Labour–Capital Partnerships and the Distribution of Risks

In the preceding section the principles of Labour–Capital Partnership were expounded by assuming that on a conversion from a fixed–wage regime to a partnership regime the shift from fixed rates of pay to a share in the firm's revenue was complete both for the capitalists and the workers. This is not at all necessary and indeed in many cases will be undesirable. Thus the partnership may well want to be free to borrow some capital funds on fixed–interest contracts with the creditors, as for example in the case of bank overdrafts; and on a shift over to the share principle some debenture or mortgage creditors of the firm may be unwilling on any terms acceptable to the partnership to convert their assets into Capital Share Certificates. On the labour side the partnership may well desire to be free to hire some forms of labour – temporary or part–time workers or consultants, for example – on fixed–wage contracts. One can also well imagine a Labour–Capital Partnership requiring all new workers to start on a fixed–wage basis and only later offering them the option of converting a part or the whole of their pay into dividends on Labour Share Certificates. For, as has been suggested above, workers on a share basis would in effect be guaranteed wholly – or, as explained later in this section, in part – against the risk of unemployment; and the existing partners might well want to assure themselves of the reliability of a new worker before making any such offer.

Even more importantly some of the existing workers might prefer to remain on fixed–wage contracts and, indeed, all the workers might desire, as an insured fall–back in the case of the firm's poor performance, to remain for part of their reward on fixed–wage contracts and only for the remaining part of their reward on participation in a share of the firm's revenue. It was suggested in the preceding section that a worker who was involuntarily dismissed would nevertheless normally retain his Labour Share Certificates until the age of retirement. In this case existing shareholders would have an incentive to dismiss a worker as redundant only if they judged that what he contributed to the value of the firm's net product had fallen below the amount of the fixed–wage element in his pay, since any dividends payable to him would remain a charge on the partnership's income, whether he were made redundant or not. Thus a worker by choosing any given mix between a fixed–wage payment and a dividend on Labour Share Certificates would thereby in effect have chosen to distribute his risks in a corresponding mix between unemployment and fluctuations in the inclusive rate of pay. The higher the fixed–wage element, the greater the risk of unemployment but the lower the risk of a drop – or indeed of a rise – in his inclusive rate of pay.

In many businesses the existing workers may have a pretty shrewd idea as to which of them are regarded as least productive by the management and are, therefore, the most likely to be made redundant if a reduction in the labour force becomes necessary. Thus a known minority of workers may face an important risk of unemployment which does not threaten the majority. In such a case if the mix between a fixed wage and a share dividend had to apply equally to all workers – an arrangement which might be demanded by a trade union which insisted on a collective decision – the choice of the majority would be for a fixed wage. If, however, it were possible for individual workers to make their own choice, those most liable to redundancy would be more favourable to a variable dividend. Such a choice would give them relative security of employment; the next layer of relatively unproductive workers would now be those who risked redundancy and would thus become more favourable to the variable dividend, and so on by a domino effect the total mix would contain a larger and larger share of variable dividend.

All of these various mixes between fixed payments and share dividends in the case both of capitalists and workers, can be incorporated in the structure of a Labour–Capital Partnership. One may make use of what we have previously defined (see V.a.3) as a firm's 'accounting profit', namely the value of its total net product less expenditure on fixed interest, fixed rents, and fixed wages. Capital and Labour Share Certificates can then be issued and distributed to those who have a claim on the firm's accounting profit. The rules and activities of the partnership can then proceed on the principles discussed in the preceding section for a Pure Labour–Capital Partnership. All Share Certificates, whether Capital or Labour would receive the same rate of dividend; in effect the recipients of the accounting profit, whether capitalists or workers, would be the risk–bearing entrepreneurs.

The partnership mechanism would be unchanged, but whether or not it would carry with it to any substantial degree the advantages of the partnership principle would, of course, depend upon whether or not a substantial proportion of the incomes of workers as well as of capitalists had been transferred to the share principle.

If, however, there were a substantial shift from fixed wage to partnership shares, the advantages of the new organization could be very substantial. Many basic conflicts of interest between labour and capital in reaching decisions about employment and investment would be resolved. Decisions to expand employment so long as there were available unemployed workers would not be impeded by the need to negotiate a reduction in pay for existing workers. Any reduction in demand for the products of the industry would be met not, as in a Capitalist Wage Economy, by a reduction in employment and growth of unemployment but by a reduction in prices and in the dividends payable to all workers and capitalists. The prospects of attaining and preserving a high and stable level of employment would be greatly improved.

(d) The Implications of Security of Employment

Consider once more a Capitalist Wage Firm. Suppose this firm to be in equilibrium: the marginal revenue product of labour (λ) is equal to the wage rate paid by the firm (w') which in turn is equal to the wage payable to the labour in other competing occupations (w''), and the marginal revenue product of capital (x) is equal to the outside market hire charge (h''). The capitalists's income will be the firm's revenue (xp) less the wage cost (λl); thus it is equal to the marginal revenue product of the capital (xk) plus any structural profit ($q_s = xp - \lambda l - xk$).

Suppose now that this firm is changed overnight into a Pure Discriminating Labour–Capital Partnership. If 80 per cent of its revenue were wage income ($\lambda l/xp = .8$) and 20 per cent were capitalists' income ($(q_s + xk)/xp = .2$), then an issue of Share Certificates would be made consisting of 80 per cent Labour Share Certificates and 20 per cent Capital Share Certificates, all distributed *pro rata* to the existing individuals' incomes from the firm. The firm will remain in equilibrium with no change.

Suppose then that there is an increase in the demand for the firm's product, with a consequent rise in the marginal revenue products of both labour and capital, but with the ouside market charges for labour and capital (w'' and h'') remaining unchanged. Employment will be increased by hiring more workers with issues of new Labour Share Certificates which entitle each worker to a dividend equal to the wage at which he can be attracted to the firm (w''). Employment will be expanded in this way until the marginal revenue product of labour has once more been reduced to the level of the outside wage ($\lambda = w''$). Similarly, investment in new capital will take place until the marginal revenue product of capital is restored to its old level ($x = h''$).

As far as the expansion of employment and investment is concerned, the resulting equilibrium will be the same in the case of the Discriminating Labour–Capital Partnership as in the case of the Capitalist Wage Firm. But the effects on the distribution of the firm's revenue between wage–income and profit–income will be very different.

We may assume that, before there is any increase in output, the increased demand will lead to an increase in the firm's selling price. In the Capitalist Wage Economy the whole of the resulting increased revenue will accrue to the capitalists' profits; in the case of a Pure Discriminating Labour–Capital Partnership, an x per cent increase in the selling price will lead to an x per cent increased dividend on all Share Certificates and thus cause the increased revenue to be shared *pro rata* between workers' income and capitalists' income. In both cases there will then be an increased output as additional amounts of both labour and capital are hired at the existing market rates (w'' and h'') until their marginal products (λ and x) have fallen to these levels. Any resulting increased revenue over and above the market price of these additional factors will also accrue solely to the capitalist's profit in the case of the Capitalist Wage Economy, but will be paid in higher dividends *pro rata* to the existing workers as well as to the existing capitalists in the case of the Discriminating Labour–Capital Partnership.

The result so far will be that in the former case the whole of the increased structural profit resulting from the increased demand for the firm's product will be added to capitalists' profit leaving the rate of pay of the existing workers unchanged at the unchanged market rate (w''); but in the latter case some part of the increased profit will have accrued to the existing workers and their inclusive rate of pay will have been raised above the market level ($w' > w''$), and security of employment means that they cannot simply for that reason be dismissed and replaced by cheaper outsiders.

However, as the existing workers retire it will pay all remaining shareholders, whether workers or capitalists, to engage new substitutes at the lower market rate (w''). The excess of the saved pay of the retired worker over the new pay of the new worker ($w' - w''$) will add to the accounting profit available for distribution on all existing Share Certificates. By this process the whole of the profit will gradually accrue to the capitalists, because the amount of Capital Share Certificates is not reduced, whereas the amount of Labour Share Certificates is continually reduced as long as the number of Share Certificates surrendered by a retiring worker is replaced by the issue of a smaller number to the lower–paid new worker. This process will go on until the incomes of all the workers are reduced to the outside market rate of pay; and at that point the distribution of income in the Discriminating Labour–Capital Partnership will be the same as in the Capitalist Wage Economy.

This distinction between the temporary, but possibly prolonged, effects of an increased demand for the firm's product on the distribution of income in the Capitalist Wage Economy and the Discriminating Labour–Capital Partnership does not work in the same way in reverse when the demand for the firm's product falls. For in this case workers are free to leave both types of employment if the pay earned in the firm falls below the outside available rate of pay ($w' < w''$). The incomes of the existing workers are to this extent safeguarded against a fall in the Discriminating Labour–Capital Partnership as much as in the Capitalist Wage Economy.

Consider next the following story. Suppose the firm to start in the same equilibrium position but with the sole difference that the outside market rate of pay at which labour can be hired is below both the firm's marginal revenue product and its inclusive rate of pay ($w'' < w' = \lambda$). This could have come about either (1) because the outside rate of pay (w'') had fallen or else (2) because the monopoly bargaining pressure of the workers had pushed up the internal rate of pay above the outside market rate ($w' > w''$) with a consequential reduction in employment until the marginal revenue product of labour was raised up to the new and higher rate of pay ($\lambda = w'$).

In both cases (1) and (2) the Discriminating Labour–Capital Partnership will expand until the marginal revenue product of labour has been reduced to the outside rate of pay ($\lambda = w''$). The existing workers and the existing capitalists will, however, experience no substantial change in their existing incomes.[1] The Capitalist Wage Firm will, however, experience very different outcomes in the two cases.

If, as in case (2), the problem is due to a monopoly bargaining position in which the inside wage (w') is fixed at a higher level than the outside wage (w''), there will be no increase in employment and output and no change in any incomes in the Capitalist Wage Firm. But if as in case (1) the labour market is perfectly competitive, the Capitalist Wage Firm will expand output in the same way as the Discriminating Labour–Capital Partnership up to the point at which the marginal revenue product of labour has fallen to the new and lower outside wage rate; but this lower wage will apply to all the existing workers and there will be a shift of income from the existing workers to the capitalists. This shift would be avoided in the Discriminating Labour–Capital Partnership because of the security of employment of the workers. The existing workers would continue to receive the higher income on their existing Share Certificates and could not be dismissed and replaced by other workers simply because they were being paid more than the outside rate of pay at which alternative workers were available.

However, as the existing high–paid workers retire, they can be replaced by the lower–paid workers to the advantage of all remaining shareholders, whether workers or capitalists, since the difference between the surrendered income of the high–paid retired worker and

[1] There will be some increase due to the sharing of any 'rent' earned on the additional output due to the fact that the first instalments of the increase in employment will earn marginal revenue products which exceed the outside rate of pay ($\lambda > w''$) while the final instalments of the increase in employment will earn only as much as the outside rate of pay ($\lambda = w''$).

the lower income of the newly employed worker will be available to add to the accounting profit available for distribution on all existing Share Certificates. Gradually the process of replacement of higher– by lower–paid workers will shift the distribution of the net product to the capitalists, since their Share Certificates are not liable to be surrendered but will gradually accumulate the whole of the profit due to the replacement of higher– by lower–paid workers. Thus in the end the equilibrium distribution of income will be the same as it would be in a Capitalist Wage Firm which was free to replace higher–paid by lower–paid workers.

Once again the distinction between the reactions of a Capitalist Wage Economy and of a Discriminating Labour–Capital Partnership does not work in reverse. Suppose that the outside wage (w''), instead of falling below, rises above the existing inside rate of pay (w'). In both forms of enterprise labour can resign its employment, leave the firm, and move to higher–paid jobs elsewhere. In the Discriminating Labour–Capital Partnership, as soon as workers had resigned in sufficient numbers to raise the marginal revenue product of labour up to, or above, the higher outside wage ($\lambda > w''$), it would pay all the shareholders, whether workers or capitalists, to issue additional Labour Share Certificates to the remaining workers in order to retain their services.

There is thus some bias introduced by the security of employment provided in a Discriminating Labour–Capital Partnership. Since labour is free to move away if it is to labour's advantage to do so but cannot be dismissed simply because it is to capitalists' advantage, the expectation of profit on capital investment will *pro tanto* be reduced by the principle of security of employment below what it would be in a Capitalist Wage Firm if that firm were able to engage its workers in a free competitive labour market. It is true that there will be a gradual restoration of the capitalists' income in the Discriminating Labour–Capital Partnership as high–paid workers retire and are replaced by lower–paid outsiders; but this process may be prolonged.

The nature of this gradual process is perhaps best understood by means of a simple numerical example, which is provided in Table VI.d.1.

Consider a firm starting in equilibrium with a revenue of £300 of which 20 per cent or £60 is accruing to the capitalist and 80 per cent or £240 is shared equally by three individual workers, L_1, L_2, and L_3, each of whom is receiving £80. The firm is a Pure Discriminating Labour–

Table VI.d.1

	Individual Workers			*All Workers*	*All Capitalists*	*Total*	*Dividend*
Year 1	L_1	L_2	L_3				
Share Certificates	80	80	80	240	60	300	$\frac{£300}{300} = £1$
Income £	80	80	80	240	60	300	–
Year 2	L_2	L_3	L_4				
Share Certificates	80	80	40	200	60	260	$\frac{£300}{260} = £1.154$
Income £	92	92	46	230	70	300	–
Year 3	L_3	L_4	L_5				
Share Certificates	80	40	35	155	60	215	$\frac{£300}{215} = £1.398$
Income £	112	56	48	216	84	300	–
Year 4	L_4	L_5	L_6				
Share Certificates	40	35	29	104	60	164	$\frac{£300}{164} = £1.837$
Income £	73	64	53	190	110	300	–
Year 7	L_7	L_8	L_9				
Share Certificates	22	19	17	58	60	118	$\frac{£300}{118} = £2.534$
Income £	55	49	44	148	152	300	–

Note: The quantitites are rounded to the nearest whole number.

Capital Partnership and this distribution of the revenue is being achieved by a dividend of £1 on each of 300 Share Certificates of which 60 are held by the capitalists and 240 by the three workers. Suppose that one worker retires every year and that at the end of year one the outside rate of pay falls from £80 to £40.

At the beginning of year two L_1 who has retired is replaced by a new worker L_4. He is attracted to the firm by the issue of 40 Share Certificates which at the dividend of £1 ruling in year one would have offered him the outside wage of £40. There are now only 200 instead of 240 Labour Share Certificates plus the unchanged 60 Capital Share Certificates. The rate of dividend earned from the same total revenue of £300 is thus in year two raised from £1 to £300/260 = £1.154. At this rate of dividend the three workers now get a total income of £92 + £92 + £46 = £230 instead of the £240 earned in year one, while the capitalists' income goes up from £60 to £70.

In year three, L_2 is replaced by L_5 to whom 35 Share Certificates are issued since these would earn £40 at the ruling rate of dividend of £1.154 per Share Certificate. There are now only 155 + 60 = 215 Share Certificates which yield a dividend of £300/215 = £1.398. At this rate of dividend the workers' total income has fallen to £216 and the capitalists' has risen to £84.

And so the process would continue until the income of the workers was reduced to £120 (i.e. to £40 per head) and the capitalists' income had risen to £180 (i.e. £300 – £120). The speed with which the new equilibrium would be reached would be the greater, (1) the greater the rate of normal turnover of the labour force and (2) the more capital–intensive the nature of the firm's activities and thus the larger the proportion of any reduction of labour cost which would pass directly to the capitalists. The process could clearly be a prolonged one.

But, against this, two considerations must be borne in mind. In the first place, the process of replacement of high cost by low cost labour in a Capitalist Wage Firm would be immediate and costless only if there were a perfectly competitive labour market. In the world of imperfect, monopolistic labour markets, the process could also be costly and prolonged, and indeed might not occur at all. Secondly, there would in the case of the Discriminating Labour–Capital Partnership be nothing to prevent new enterprises being formed on the basis of the cheaper labour and thus entering into competition with the existing enterprise, whose revenue available for distribution on existing Share Certificates would thus be cut. The dividend incomes of the existing working partners would *pro tanto* be automatically reduced towards the level prevailing outside.

Consider next the following story. We start once again with the same firm in the same conditions of full equilibrium. Suppose now that there is a labour–saving invention. Consider the extreme form of such an invention whereby a robot is invented to do exactly the same work as a man but in conditions in which the market rate of pay of a man is £10 ($w'' =$ £10) while the market hire–charge for the capital needed for the purchase of a robot is only £6 ($h'' =$ £6).

In a Capitalist Wage Firm employing labour in a perfectly competitive labour market men will be dismissed as redundant and replaced by robots, thus saving £4 (£10 – £6) on each replacement.

In a Discriminating Labour–Capital Partnership the men's pay in so far as it takes the form of a dividend on Labour Share Certificates, cannot be saved in this way by dismissal on grounds of redundancy.

Such substitution may, however, take place in a Partial Partnership. Suppose, for example, that of a man's pay of £10, £7 is a fixed wage and £3 is a dividend on Labour Share Certificates. Then the substitution of a man by a robot will reduce costs by £1 from £10 (the original pay of the man) to £9, i.e. the sum of £6 (the hire–charge of the robot) plus £3 (the continuing dividend payment to the redundant man). All the shareholders (including the redundant man) would stand to gain by the higher rate of dividend payable on Share Certificates as a result of the saving of cost.

If, however, the share–dividend element in the man's pay of £10 had been anything greater than £4, it would not pay to replace the man with a robot. If, for example, the share–dividend element in his inclusive pay of £10 had been £5, the cost after the replacement of the man by the robot would have risen from £10 to £6 + £5 = £11. All shareholders would stand to lose by the substitution.

In this latter case the replacement of men by robots will be held up until the individual man reaches the age of retirement, at which point the firm's liability to pay the dividend on the man's Share Certificates will cease. At this point it will pay the remaining shareholders to replace the man by a robot and to enjoy the higher rate of dividend on Share Certificates which is made possible by the saving in cost.[1]

[1] Table VI.d.1 can be used to illustrate the case in which L_1, L_2, L_3 represent existing workers whose pay is £80 being replaced in a Pure Discriminating Labour–Capital Partnership on retirement by robots, L_4, L_5, L_6 whose 'cost' is £40. In year two the original Capital Shareholders receive £70, the new Capital Shareholders who have financed the first robot (L_4) receive £46 in dividends, and the two remaining workers (L_2 and L_3) receive £92 + £92. In year three the original capitalists receive £84, the new capitalists receive £56 + £48 on their Share Certificates, and the remaining worker, L_3, receives £112. In year four the original capitalists receive £110 and the new capitalists who have financed the installation of the robots receive £190; and this situation then continues indefinitely, since robots do not retire but continue indefinitely to produce a net output (after allowing for their depreciation) equal to a workers' output.

In a Capitalist Wage Firm which could freely replace men with robots, the labour share of the firm's revenue would have fallen abruptly from 80% in year one to zero in year two. In Table VI.d.1 this ratio falls gradually in the following way:

Year 1	(80 + 80 + 80)/300	= 80%
Year 2	(92 + 92)/300	= 61.3%
Year 3	112/300	= 37.3%
Year 4	0/300	= 0%

But consider a Capitalist Wage Firm which has financed most of its capital through long-term fixed-interest debt and which is then faced with a serious fall in the demand for its product. It may then be forced to allocate to capital an abnormally high proportion of its reduced revenue. Is the security of return to Labour-Share-Certificate work under the partnership principle more anomalous than the security of return to Fixed-Interest capital in a Capitalist Wage Firm?

In addition to the immediate installation of robots to replace men whose pay includes only a small element of dividend on Share Certificates and in addition to the gradual installation of robots to replace other men as they reach the age of retirement, there is, of course, nothing to prevent the immediate installation of robots in new firms which are set up in order to take advantage of the cost reduction and so to compete on favourable terms with old firms which continue to employ men rather than robots. In this case the market for the products of the old firms will contract, the accounting profit made in such firms will fall, and the dividends on existing Share Certificates will be reduced. As a result men may voluntarily leave such firms as their inclusive rate of pay falls below what they can earn elsewhere, and they can then be replaced by robots.

In the Capitalist Wage Firm operating in a perfectly competitive labour market the replacement of men by robots would not depend at all upon the competition of new firms; it would occur perhaps with even greater ease in the existing firms. To this extent the restoration of full equilibrium through the mechanism of entry of new firms is of greater importance in the case of Discriminating Labour–Capital Partnerships than in the case of Capitalist Wage Firms; its importance is, however, not as great as we found it to be in the case of Non–Discriminating Labour Co–operatives where (see Section (e) of Chapter IV) ease of entry is of basic importance for the general maintenance of equilibrium.

Our fairy story about robots which are exact and cheap substitutes for men is, of course, only an extreme case of technological change which has the effect of raising the marginal product of capital equipment relative to the marginal product of labour. In imperfect competition where the total market for an individual firm's output is limited, such technological changes may make it economic to dismiss labour in order to replace such labour with an investment in additional capital equipment. In such a case the installation of new technologies may be slowed up in a Discriminating Labour–Capital Partnership in the way illustrated by our fairy tale about the wicked robots. Final equilibrium in such a case of labour–saving incentives will imply a higher real national product but a shift of its distribution relatively away from the pay of labour to the return on capital. Labour–Capital Partnerships, just as Capitalist Wage Firms, are not designed to do anything fundamental about these underlying factors which determine the long–run distribution of income between labour–income and capital–income. Long–run redistribution of the income from property must rely on other institutional and policy reforms.

We may summarize the analysis in this section in the following way. The principle of security of employment in a Discriminating Labour–Capital Partnership will (1) introduce some bias against the expectation of profit on capital investment since labour will be free to leave at once if it turns out to be underpaid but will not necessarily be liable to be dismissed if it turns out to be overpaid and (2) where technological developments would make it profitable to replace labour by capital equipment, the substitution may be delayed.

Whether or not these considerations tell against the organization of Discriminating Labour–Capital Partnerships depends upon the degree of imperfection in the labour market. If such imperfection is great, there may be as serious or even more serious obstacles impeding and delaying the adjustment of rates of pay for workers in Capitalist Wage Firms. In this case the fact that discrimination will make it easier to replace high–paid retiring workers with lower–paid outsiders may mean that in the end adjustment is easier and quicker in the Discriminating Labour–Capital partnership. But the organization of a Discriminating Labour–Capital Partnership may well introduce some net disincentive to invest, which would need to be offset as far as possible by a reduction in the cost of borrowing capital funds and so in the hire–charge for capital equipment (h''); and in assessing the relative merits of the two forms of enterprise any such disincentive to the commitment of new capital funds to Discriminating Labour–Capital Partnerships would need to be balanced against other possible advantages resulting from the partnership principle.

(e) Some Remaining Conflicts of Interest

For the reasons given in Section (b) of this chapter many basic conflicts of interest between capitalists and workers about decisions affecting the levels of employment, investment, and output would be avoided in a Labour–Capital Partnership. Indeed, the whole object of the institution would be to enable all partners, capitalists and workers, to bear the risks and enjoy the fruits of success in the business; and this would for the most part be achieved by the principle that the dividend paid on Capital Share Certificates would be the same as the dividend paid on Labour Share Certificates, with the consequence that any decision which is to the advantage of the one type of partner will be to the advantage also of the other. There are, however, certain inevitable exceptions to this general rule.

One obvious case would be a decision to devote part of the firm's resources to the provision of social amenities or fringe benefits of a type (such as canteen facilities) which would be valued by the workers but which would not confer any direct benefits on the owners of the capital invested in the business.

A more serious and direct conflict of interest could arise from decisions to promote workers from one grade to a higher grade of work, a decision which would involve the issue of additional Labour Share Certificates to the promoted workers. Promotions are, of course, a proper and desirable phenomenon – indeed, a necessary one if able persons are to be retained in the firm's service in which case the promotion would, of course, be of ultimate benefit to all shareholders. But they could in theory be misused; if they were made on a wholesale scale which was unnecessary for the success of the firm's activities, they would result simply in a shift of part of the revenue of the firm from Capital Shareholders to Labour Shareholders.

The basic distinction between Labour Share Certificates and Capital Share Certificates is that the former give entitlement to dividend income until retiring age while the latter give an entitlement to a dividend income for the indefinite future. This distinction between an annuity and a perpetuity can give rise to a conflict of interest. A worker, particularly a worker near retiring age, is naturally less concerned than is a holder of Capital Share Certificate with the effect of management decisions on the future fortunes of the firm and is more concerned with their more immediate present effects.

Arrangements could be made which would satisfactorily avoid conflicts of interest arising from this distinction, if it were possible always to adopt an accounting procedure which would give a clear and unequivocal definition of what was the firm's accounting profit in any period, in the sense of the amount of dividends that could be distributed to the shareholders and yet leave enough funds to ensure that the capital resources of the firm were so maintained as to allow this same level of accounting profit to be sustained indefinitely in the future. If less were distributed, then capital resources would be more than maintained so that some part of current accounting profit should be treated as a net saving by the firm. If more were distributed in dividends, then the firm would be dissaving and living on its capital to that extent.

In these conditions any decision on the part of the management not to distribute in dividends the whole of the firm's distributable accounting profit but to use part of it to finance a capital development or to build up a reserve of liquid assets, need not cause a basic clash of interest between workers and capitalists if it were properly managed. An appropriate arrangement would be that there should be an issue of additional Capital Share Certificates equal at current valuations to the amount of distributable accounting profit which was not distributed in dividend, and that these additional Capital Share Certificates instead of being sold in the market should be distributed in lieu of dividend *pro rata* to all existing shareholders whether workers or capitalists. Thus workers as well as capitalists would acquire Capital Share Certificates (which they would be perfectly free to hold or to sell as they chose), to represent that part of the firm's income which had been held back from distribution on their existing Share Certificates. There might even so remain some conflict of interest if workers desired more than capitalists to receive immediate payment in dividends rather than a participation in the growth of the capital value of the business. It would, however, be possible to arrange for the dividend on Capital Share Certificates to be cut without cutting the dividend on Labour Share Certificates and to issue the additional Capital Share Certificates solely to the existing holders of such certificates, so that it was only the capitalists who financed the ploughing back of revenue into an expansion of the capital resources of the business.

The choice of appropriate definition of the distinction between available income and the capital resources needed to maintain income is difficult enough and the subsequent choice of appropriate accounting procedures to apply that definition greatly increases the difficulty, particularly in inflationary conditions when a depreciation allowance has properly to be set at a level which will in some sense replace the real effective amount of capital equipment rather than merely meet its old historic money cost. For many reasons it is not always easy to find a crisp, clear, and unequivocal answer to the basic question; 'Of sums set aside from the gross revenue of the firm how much truly represents a provision to maintain the real capital resources of the firm intact and how much in fact serves to increase the real capital resources of the firm?' An unduly low estimation of the sums which should be put aside for depreciation would cause an overestimation of the amount of distributable accounting profit that was being withheld from distribution and would thus confer on the Labour Shareholders an issue of Capital Share Certificates to which they had no legitimate claim, or would impose on Capital Shareholders an exceptional charge on their dividends which was not really justified. An unduly high estimate of the deductions from gross revenue needed to meet capital depreciation would have the opposite kind of effect.

It is not intended in this book to consider in depth the problems of definition of what constitutes true sustainable income. The following is simply one example of a problem which might arise of a kind which would be likely to cause a conflict of interest between holders of Labour and holders of Capital Share Certificates. Suppose the management were confronted with the possibility of replacing part of the firm's capital equipment with equipment based on a new technology which would admittedly not produce a very high return in the near future period of inevitable teething troubles but which *might*, if successful, produce an exceedingly high return in future years. The holders of Labour Share Certificates – and in particular those near retiring age – would have every justification in demanding that an accounting procedure should be adopted which treated the low returns expected during the immediate low years as due to savings which were being made in order to lead to the uncertain, but hoped for, high returns of the successive years. But quite what allowances should be made for the uncertainty surrounding these venturesome new technologies and what rates of discount should be used to evaluate them in order to make the relevant calculations, would be a matter for somewhat arbitrary choices.

Indeed the basic attitudes to risk of worker shareholders and of capitalist shareholders may differ and this could in itself lead to some conflict of interest. Since capital shareholders are able to spread their holding of shares over a large number of enterprises, they may be more ready to promote risky activities in any one of the businesses in which they hold an interest; they can in fact spread their risks widely. Worker shareholders cannot spread the risks attached to their pay for work done, since it is not possible for them to spread their work over a large number of independent businesses; being unable to spread their risks, they may be more risk averse than the capital shareholders in regard to the choice of activities in which the enterprise should take part. Workers may favour safe rather then risky investment of the firm's resources; and for this reason the introduction of the workers into the entrepreneurial function may lead to some clash of interest and to some brake upon new and risky developments.

There is one further source of trouble which should be mentioned. It has been proposed that a worker who leaves the firm voluntarily to seek a better–paid job should surrender his Labour Share Certificates, whereas a worker who is dismissed as redundant should retain them. It would thus be in the interest of a worker who wished to move elsewhere to be dismissed as redundant rather than himself to resign his membership of the partnership. For this purpose he might make himself as useless as possible, indeed perhaps as tiresome as possible, to the management without stepping over the borderline which would justify his dismissal for misconduct with consequential surrender of his Labour Share Certificates. The conflict of interest in this case would be between the delinquent worker on the one hand and all other shareholders on the other hand; but there is clearly here the possibility of tiresome disputes requiring judgement by some form of industrial tribunal.

(f) Participation in Decision–Making

It is clear that the organization of a Discriminating Labour–Capital Partnership on the lines described in the preceding sections of this chapter would remove many of the basic causes of conflict between labour and capital which might otherwise arise. To the extent that this is so, the way would be open for a true partnership between labour and capital in sharing the fruits of success or failure in the business and in participating together in the decisions about levels of employment, investment, output, sale prices, and so on. In the absence of any possible sources of conflict of the kind discussed in Section (e) the simplest arrangement would be to achieve full partnership by the provision that every Share Certificate, whether Labour or Capital, should give an entitlement not only to the same rate of dividend but also to the same voting power at shareholders' meetings.

While one–share–one–vote would be the simplest arrangement it is not necessarily the best even if there were no potential conflicts of interest of the kind discussed in Section (e). Suppose a managerial mistake is made which involves a lasting loss of £1 a year in dividend on every Share Certificate. A worker who is about to retire next year loses this £1 for one year; a young worker who has a working life of thirty years till retirement loses it for the next thirty years; a holder of a Capital Share Certificate and his heirs lose this amount in perpetuity. If r is the relevant rate of discount, there is a loss of £$1/r$ on every Capital Share Certificate and a loss of £$(1/r\{1 - 1/(1+r)^n\}$ on a Labour Share Certificate where n measures the remaining number of working years for the particular holder of the Labour Share Certificate. It might be considered fair to weight the number of votes to which each Share Certificate gave entitlement by some such formula to represent the present value of the future stake which each shareholder had in the fortunes of the firm.[1]

But weighted voting of this kind, while it might be appropriate for decision–making about matters in which there was no basic clash of interests between Workers and Capitalists as such would not meet the problem of resolving such direct conflicts of interest as were described in Section (e). Such conflicts (e.g. about the use or misuse of promotion procedures or about the appropriate accounting procedures to assess the true sustainable income of the firm) are not properly resolved by allowing the choice simply to go one way or another according to the voting strength of the one party or the other, a voting strength which would be affected not only by the question whether the votes allotted to each Share Certificate should be weighted in some way (for example, as described in the preceding paragraph), but also by the extent to which the firm in question was in a labour–intensive or a capital–intensive activity and by the extent to which labour and capital had each retained fixed–wage or fixed–interest elements in their contracts of employment. Conflicts of the kind discussed in Section (e) require a solution based on their merits, not on the voting power of adversaries. To resolve such conflicts of interest it might be wise for a partnership to rule that certain decisions on issues of the kind discussed in Section (e) – or indeed that all decisions – would require the agreement of representatives of both types of partner or, in the case of dispute, would be referred to some form of agreed arbitration. In any case it is clear that Labour–Capital Partnerships of the kind discussed in this chapter could work only in a general atmosphere of mutual trust in which the partners wished to make the partnership work and were prepared to accept some machinery for sensible compromise in any such cases of dispute.

[1] I owe this suggestion to J. S. Flemming.

(g) The Implications of the Principle of Discrimination

The institutional arrangements for a Labour–Capital Partnership differ in one very important respect from those for all of the other three institutions analysed in this book. The Capitalist Wage Firm, the Non–Discriminating Labour Co–operative, and the Capitalist Revenue–Sharing Firm are all based on the principle of non–discrimination in the sense that workers of the same grade working together in the same firm will all receive the same pay on the principle of 'equal pay for equal work'. This principle is not observed in the Labour–Capital Partnerships discussed in this chapter.

It is helpful to contrast the relationship between employment and rate of pay in the Capitalist Wage Firm and in the Capitalist Revenue–Sharing Firm with the relationship between employment and rate of pay in a Discriminating Labour–Capital Partnership. In all cases it is assumed in our model that the marginal revenue product of labour will fall as a firm employs more labour. This is so for two reasons. First, the assumed production function is such that the marginal product of labour is assumed to fall as more labour is applied to a given amount of capital (see II.c.4). Second, the product is assumed to be sold in an imperfect market so that the firm will have to cut its selling price in order to sell the increased product (see II.a.8).

In the Capitalist Wage Firm this means that in order to make it possible to find employment for additional workers in any given state of market demand for the product it is necessary to reduce the money wage rate, a reduction which on the principle of non–discrimination will apply to all workers, new and old, (see III.b.18).

In the Capitalist Revenue–Sharing Firm the same analysis applies in so far as the wage parameters s and w are flexible and are confidently expected to be flexible. For in these conditions (see the discussion of V.f.5) the firm will employ labour up to the point at which the inclusive rate of pay is equal to the marginal revenue product of labour and the same inclusive rate of pay will be paid to all workers on the principle of non–discrimination.

At the same time in the short run so long as the wage parameters s and w remained fixed in the current wage contract, an employer would be willing to take on any additional worker who offered his or her services. As a result of taking on additional workers the average revenue per worker of the firm would fall, both because output per head would fall as more workers were applied to the same capital eqquipment and also because the firm would have to cut its price in order to sell the additional output. As a result of the fall in revenue per worker the share element in every worker's inclusive rate of pay (namely sxp/l) would fall and so the inclusive rate of pay would automatically be reduced for all workers on the principle of non–discrimination.

There is, however, the following important distinction. In the Capitalist Wage Firm there has to be a deliberate and conscious modification of an existing wage contract, it being clearly recognized by every worker that the wage rate is being reduced; but in the Capitalist Revenue–Sharing Firm with an unchanged pay parameter s the reduction of inclusive pay occurs for all existing workers automatically as a result of the employment of the additional workers and without any express modification of an existing wage contract.

In the Discriminating Labour–Capital Partnership when an additional number of workers is employed, they will be paid a reward in the form of a fixed wage or an expected dividend on newly issued Labour Share Certificates which is related to the lower marginal revenue product of labour which results from the increase in employment. But this will not affect the dividends on the Labour Share Certificates of the existing workers. The newly employed workers may in that case receive a lower income from the firm than do the existing workers. The non–discriminating principle of 'equal pay for equal work' will not necessarily be observed.

Consider a partnership starting in full equilibrium with all worker partners receiving the same earnings at a rate equal to what they could earn elsewhere. Any outside newcomer who replaces a retiring partner in these circumstances will be admitted on the same terms as the existing insiders. Suppose, however, that for some reason or another the partnership fares badly, either because the demand for its particular brand of product declines or else because the efficiency with which the concern is managed deteriorates. The existing worker partners will share the loss; their earnings will fall below what can be earned elsewhere; but they will not risk the loss of these reduced earnings by being made redundant without pay. Any existing partner will, however, be free to leave the partnership if he can find a better–paid job elsewhere; and in so doing he would restore his income to the higher outside level without sharing the resulting improvement in his pay with any of the other partners, whether workers or capitalists, who remain at their depressed earnings in the old partnership.

The position of the capitalist shareholders in a depressed partnership is different. Suppose that as a result of the depressed demand for the partnership's product the rate of earnings on a machine employed in the partnership had fallen from 10 per cent (the rate available in other outside uses) to 5 per cent. It would now pay the partnership as a whole to hire out the machine at a 10 per cent return for use elsewhere; or, to take the more realistic case in which the machine itself could not so readily be switched to other uses, it would pay the partnership as a whole to use the depreciation allowance on the machine as it wore out not for the replacement of the machine, but for investment outside the partnership in some way which would earn the going rate of 10 per cent. But, given the way in which a discriminating capital market is organized (see the note at the end of Chapter I), any advantage gained by this avoidance of the depressed 'pay' of the machine would not accrue to any particular capitalist shareholder as if he individually owned this particular machine; it would accrue as an increase in the accounting profit available for the support of the dividends paid on all Share Certificates, that is to say, in the interests of worker partners as well as of capitalist partners. Unexpected loss ultimately settles on the capitalists who commit their capital resources on a perpetuity basis; it rests on workers only so long as they can, or must, or choose to commit their labour to the partnership.

Consider next the opposite case in which the partnership does exceptionally well because of an increase in the demand for its product or because of an exceptionally efficient productive effort. The existing worker partners will share the increased accounting profit with the existing capitalist partners. Moreover (see the numerical example in Table VI.d.1), as and when newcomers are admitted from outside at lower outside rates of pay to replace retiring members, the remaining original worker partners will add still more to their share of the profit; and each newcomer as time passes will himself enjoy a growing profit as more and more old hands retire and surrender their profit to be shared among all shareholders.

It is true, as explained in Section (d), that the whole gain will in the end seep away from the body of worker partners to the benefit of the capital shareholders, who stand ultimately to enjoy the gains just as they stand (though rather more promptly) to bear any losses. But as can be seen from Table V.d.1, this seepage of the gains will be a prolonged process. In the first place, all the originally existing worker partners will obtain and retain until retirement their share of any lasting improvement of profit made by the partnership. Second, as some of the original partners retire, all the remaining original worker partners will share further in the profit surrendered by the retiring worker partners. Third so long as any profit remains in the enjoyment of the worker partners (and it will be a long time before the worker profit seeps entirely away), outsiders who join the partnership at the outside going rate of pay will have the prospect of receiving a growing profit supplement to their earnings which, provided that the partnership maintains its favourable position, they will retain until their own retirement.

The strict principle of 'equal pay for equal work' will not be preserved. But 'new hands' joining a successful partnership in which the 'old hands' are enjoying a rate of earnings in excess of the outside rate of pay will have the prospect of themselves becoming 'old hands' as time passes and of enjoying a substantial part, though not the whole, of the privileged position of the existing 'old hands'. The advantages of the application of the principle of discrimination to the employment of the unemployed outsiders rests upon the acceptability of this degree of modification of the principle of equal pay for equal work.

(h) Concluding Observations on Discriminating Labour–Capital Partnerships

No system is perfect. All economists should learn to be ambidextrous and to explain, on the one hand, the disadvantages and, on the other hand, the advantages of their proposals.

It is difficult to conceive of a full partnership between labour and capital which does not give some degree of security of tenure to the worker partners. This, as we saw in Section (d) is bound to introduce some extra risk for capital investment, some bias against risky investments in particular, and some delays in the introduction of innovations which are seriously labour–saving. This set of disadvantages should not be overstressed, since trade union or similar pressure is in any case likely to impede similar disturbing changes in the wage economy as it works in reality, and it is possible that in some respects the impediments would be even more serious in the wage economy than in the partnership economy.

Some serious conflicts of interest could, as we saw in Section (e), still persist in any conceivable partnership, particularly in connection with the definition and interpretation of what constituted the real sustainable income of the partnership; and there would also be tiresome difficulties in defining and enforcing the conditions on which a worker partner's uncompensated dismissal was justified.

It is, however, claimed (see Section (b)) that many of the main conflicts of interest between labour and capital could be removed by the introduction of flexible shares and that important obstacles to full employment could be removed through the principle of discrimination between 'old hands' and 'new hands'. These advantages depend, however, upon two basic conditions: first, the acceptance of the necessary modifications of the strict principle of 'equal pay for equal work' (discussed in Section (g)); and, second, the willingness of workers to participate in bearing risks of variations in the firm's revenue, a willingness which might be promoted by the possibility of choosing a mix between risks of unemployment and risks of variations of income, as outlined in Section (c).

Discriminating Labour–Capital Partnerships, if in spite of these obstacles their promotion should prove possible, would have all the basic partnership features (namely, the possible improvements in industrial relations due to breaking down the distinction between 'them' and 'us') organized in a way which would greatly ease the problem of stagflation.

First, the share principle would mean that the impact effect of any fall in demand would be upon a concern's money prices and incomes rather than taking the basically wasteful form of a reduction in employment and real output.

Second, the principle of discrimination would remove much of the conflict between 'insiders' and 'outsiders'. Those already in employment in any successful partnership would not be required to face a reduction in their pay as a necessary condition for allowing unemployed outsiders to join in the concern's useful activities.

There are serious obstacles, but there is much to be gained.

Select Bibliography

Chamberlin, E. H. (1933), *The Theory of Monopolistic Competition* (Cambridge, Mass.: Harvard University Press).

Vanek, J. (1970), *The General Theory of Labor-Managed Market Economies* (Ithaca, NY: Cornell University Press).

Weitzman, M. L. (1984), *The Share Economy* (Cambridge, Mass.: Harvard University Press).

Index

For Product Safety Concerns and Information please contact our EU
representative GPSR@taylorandfrancis.com
Taylor & Francis Verlag GmbH, Kaufingerstraße 24, 80331 München, Germany

www.ingramcontent.com/pod-product-compliance
Lightning Source LLC
LaVergne TN
LVHW021111300926
849160LV00009B/685